Advance Praise for
The Relatable Leader

"In *The Relatable Leader,* Rachel DeAlto dismantles outdated leadership assumptions and reveals how relatability—rooted in trust, communication, and inspiration—is the key to unlocking potential in teams and organizations. Through proprietary research, peer-reviewed studies, and real-world experiences, she provides actionable strategies to help leaders foster cultures of respect, psychological safety, and connection. This book is an essential guide for leaders who want to move beyond *traditional authority and create workplaces where people thrive.*"

LAURA GASSNER OTTING, ABC Contributor and
Wall Street Journal bestselling author

"In an era where AI is transforming the workplace, one truth remains: leadership is decidedly human. *The Relatable Leader* is the guide every leader needs to navigate the future of work, where trust, communication, and authenticity are the competitive edge that AI can't replicate. Rachel DeAlto delivers a research-backed blueprint for building connected, high-performing teams in a world where technology is accelerating change—but human connection drives success."

DR. SHAWN DUBRAVAC, *New York Times*
bestselling author

"*The Relatable Leader* is the book I didn't know I needed to read to get me to where I want to go next. With a perfect mix of science and story, this book gave me exactly what I needed while enjoying every page. This book should be considered a foundational tool for those looking to be the leader they dreamed of being."

ERIC TERMUENDE, author of
Rethink Work and Co-founder of NoW of Work

"Having led billion dollar campaigns in professional sports, I know firsthand that extraordinary results come from extraordinary leadership. DeAlto's *The Relatable Leader* provides exactly what today's leaders need—a winning framework for creating the kind of authentic connections that drive peak performance. Like any championship team, successful organizations are built on trust, respect, and genuine relationships. This book shows you how to develop all three. It's time to play offense with your leadership."

PAUL EPSTEIN, Former NFL & NBA Executive,
two time bestselling author of
The Power of Playing Offense and *Better Decisions Faster*

"*The Relatable Leader* provides a blueprint every leader can follow to make their teams happier and more productive. DeAlto's research-backed model for leadership strips away complexities to reveal the actionable steps that actually drive real results. Whether you're leading five people or five thousand, this book gives you the tools to create a culture where both employees and customers become loyal advocates."

BRITTANY HODAK, author of *Creating Superfans*

THE
RELATABLE
LEADER

Create a Culture of Connection

RACHEL DeALTO

Post Hill
PRESS

A POST HILL PRESS BOOK
ISBN: 979-8-88845-898-3
ISBN (eBook): 979-8-88845-899-0

The Relatable Leader:
Create a Culture of Connection
© 2025 by Rachel DeAlto
All Rights Reserved

Cover design by Jim Villaflores

Post Hill Press
New York • Nashville
posthillpress.com

Published in the United States of America
1 2 3 4 5 6 7 8 9 10

Table of Contents

Introduction

"How could someone be so callous?" I muttered under my breath. I was sitting in the gallery, the back of the courtroom, listening to an attorney meet their client for the first time. His tone was rude, pompous, and flippant all at once and was likely because the client wasn't paying the attorney's typical retainer—or any retainer, for that matter. As a lawyer in private practice, New Jersey requires that lawyers take on a certain number of pro bono assignments. Clearly, this attorney was less than pleased that the man before him wasn't going to be an easy or profitable case.

Admittedly, only a few attorneys, including myself, look forward to pro bono work. You aren't choosing your clients; the litigants are typically wary of a court-appointed counselor, and the cases were often in an area I was wholly unfamiliar with—domestic violence, parole issues, and municipal appeals. I was a civil litigator intentionally; I had no desire to step foot in criminal court. Yet, there I was, ready to meet my next client, and it took everything in me to avoid preconceived notions of who they were and how painful this experience would be—likely for both of us.

As I began working on *The Relatable Leader*, I kept returning to my time in the courthouse. Those pro bono cases taught me so much about the dangers of assumptions and the power of relatability. They showed me firsthand how easy it is to cast judgment and miss the mark when we need to take the time to understand the people we aim to serve.

How often do we, as leaders, make assumptions? How frequently do we show up the way we want to show up? What is the way we think our team wants us to be? Oh, how often we miss the mark.... We can do it better! We can become leaders who inspire loyalty and engagement through the power of *relatability*.

In over a decade of consulting, speaking, and studying human connection, I've witnessed the consequences of disconnection. I've seen how difficult it is to bridge the gap when trust is lost and assumptions are made. I've also seen the power of relatability in overcoming the hurdles of misunderstanding.

Many leaders struggle to create connections with and within their teams. How many managers do you know who would consider themselves an "accidental leader"—someone who ended up in their position due to their professional success but without the requisite professional development? How many supervisors desperately try to balance their workflow and develop their teams? The pressure can feel oppressive. It makes sense that we grasp at straws and rely on assumptions to guide our actions. But what if there was a better way?

Assumptions create barriers, while understanding builds bridges.

Leaders who relate to their teams on a human level, through creating an environment of trust, respect, and purpose, create connection cultures. Relatable leaders influence, motivate, and elevate their teams to better collaboration, more innovation, and unlocking potential.

Yet many organizations still operate on assumptions—assumptions based on the latest article or expert opinion on what leadership should look like. In *The Relatable Leader*, we'll explore what makes great leaders stand apart in a sea of disengaged workforces through proprietary research, peer-reviewed studies, and real-world experiences. I'll reveal actionable practices for creating contagious job satisfaction built on the existing pillars of relatability—connection, communication, and inspiration.

We'll start by debunking the myths surrounding connecting with our teams and what they truly seek in a leader. My proprietary research, studying 400 professionals in the US of every generation, found that while many components create a strong, relatable leader, behaviors cultivating primary psychological safety eclipse the need for vulnerability, self-awareness, and resilience. Across roles, generations, and genders, *respect* emerged as the number one trait determining leader relatability. Aretha, we should have listened to what you've been trying to tell us since 1967.

Yet respect alone does not make a relatable leader. We have to dig deeper into the behaviors and environments that allow respect to grow in the first place—environments built on psychological safety, trust, and care for the whole employee, through relatable leadership that connects teams to purpose, people to potential, and organizations to outsized results.

In the pages ahead, I'll uncover the roadmap for organizations ready to evolve from mandates to collaboration and from assumptions to understanding, for leaders prepared to show up as their best selves in service of unleashing the best in others, not through pizza or pickleball, but through relatable leaders invested in realizing human potential.

Employees are looking to do things differently. The generational landscape of our workforce is changing. What has worked before is no longer working. Employees are looking for leaders who relate to them on a human level, fostering environments of trust, respect, and purpose.

The Relatable Leader isn't just another leadership book; it's a research-driven roadmap to unlocking human potential. Embracing the actionable methods within these pages transforms disconnection and boosts your bottom line. You'll connect teams to purpose, people to potential, and organizations to results through relatable leadership.

The goal of *The Relatable Leader* is simple: Transform your leadership style to unlock your team's potential. Get ready to embrace the power of relatability and watch your team thrive in a culture of connection.

CHAPTER 1

Relatable Leadership: Tenets and Truths

"Your assumptions aren't barriers;
they're bridges to understanding waiting to be crossed."

Our barista handed me a metal stand with an order number affixed to the top, and we began searching for a spare table. The local coffee shop had taken on a cult following. Regardless of the hour, it was always humming with an eclectic mix of patrons—the work-from-home crowd trying to find a change of scenery, moms and their toddlers seeking adult conversation, and those like Jamie and I—friends catching up after what felt like years, because it *was* years. We sank into the oversized velvet chairs and nearly simultaneously said, "It's been too long!"

I had known Jamie for nearly two decades. We worked together at my job post-college and pre-law school, and while I wouldn't define us as being close, we were connected. We followed each other on social media, keeping tabs on the highlights of one another's lives, but apart from an occasional text check-in from time to time, we didn't know much about what was happening behind the screen. Me? I was under the impression Jamie was crushing it. The last time we talked, everything was going her way. Her family was happy and healthy, her husband won his fantasy football league (obviously a highlight of the decade), and she landed her dream job at a prestigious marketing agency with high-profile accounts that maintained even higher budgets.

"You first," I said as I raised my piping hot caramel macchiato to take a sip. "Well, I'm unemployed," she replied. I was so stunned I nearly dropped my cup. "What?! What happened?!" Shaking her head, Jamie started recounting the agency's goings. She loved her colleagues, but the leadership was out of touch, disconnected, and, worst of all, untrustworthy. They kept trying to get her to stay with perks and money, but it wasn't enough to make up for the fact that she felt apprehension and dread every time she walked in the door. "The final straw was when my boss took my idea for a campaign and presented it to the client and his boss as his own. You know me, I didn't keep quiet when I confronted him in front of his boss. I was told I was overreacting," she shared with the enthusiasm of someone still clearly perturbed. "Wow, that is awful. You'd think in an organization that successful, they would be held more accountable. I'd have thought the environment would be different," I replied. "One would think," she sighed. "I'm just grateful I have several other opportunities lined up—and you know I will be upping my due diligence!"

Jamie lasted eighteen months at her dream job. She was paid well, challenged, and excited by the work, but she would instead take a pay cut and work somewhere she felt valued. These scenarios play out over and over. In some cases, employees can take the risk and leave, hoping to find a job elsewhere. In others, the employee remains, but resentment and disengagement grow.

What if we could do things differently? What if leaders could work to connect with teams in the way their employees are genuinely looking for? What if being a relatable leader could retain and engage talent like Jamie?

WHY RELATABILITY

Relatability is the ability to easily connect to, communicate with, and inspire others (and ourselves). It's beyond likable. Likable means they make you comfortable enough to stand and work in close proximity. Likeable is small talk and small smiles. Likable people are nice to be around and can be easy to talk to...and that's usually as far as they go. Relatable people, on the other hand, attract investments of time and energy—you find yourself wanting to engage, listen, share, and learn with them. You feel seen by them—and you see yourself in them. You can feel the benefit of that connection, like awesome by osmosis, either in what the relationship creates or who you become because of it.

As I shared in my 2021 book, *relatable*, my first real inkling of relatability's power goes back to when I was on a show called *Married at First Sight*. Its original concept featured three couples paired by relationship experts who agree to marry when they first meet at the altar, sight unseen (the title is real!). They then live together as a married couple for six weeks—after which they must choose to stay together or get divorced. As the communication and relationship expert on the show—and long after I left it two seasons later—I received hundreds, if not thousands, of messages from people via email, X (previously Twitter), and Instagram. I was surprised they didn't show up at my doorstep! They all said the same thing—how I was such a *relatable* expert.

It got me thinking—how did people relate to me? I was a talking head on a screen to most of them. How did they get that feeling across so many pixels and miles? What is it about relatability that made them want to get to know me, to share so much about their lives, and to take the advice I was giving? And that was the question I sought to answer. I don't believe in sample sizes of one, so seven years, one master's degree, three TedX talks, hundreds of keynotes, and too many TikTok followers for someone in their forties later, I learned the secret that isn't a secret at all. The good news is that relatability isn't genetic, a special gift, or an innate superpower of a select few. Relatability is a learned skill. Relatability is a choice.

As my research continued, it became clear that relatability is the foundation of leadership. Relatability means acknowledging you don't have all the answers; creating spaces for people to feel heard and understood is at the heart of it. Relatability transforms bosses into coaches who bring out the best in their teams. Relatability is about less certainty and more curiosity.

At the core of relatability—whether in leadership, personal relationships, or any human interaction—lies the CCI Framework: *Connect*, *Communicate*, and *Inspire*. This framework, which I developed through years of research and real-world application, is the foundation for building meaningful connections in all aspects of life.

Connect is about nurturing genuine relationships and creating an environment of trust and understanding. It's the ability to see and value others for who they are, regardless of differences in background, age, or perspective.

Communicate encompasses not just the ability to express oneself clearly but also to listen actively and adapt one's communication style to engage with others in the way they are most receptive. It's about creating a two-way dialogue that bridges gaps and facilitates mutual understanding.

Inspire relates to the capacity to motivate and empower others and oneself. It's about finding and sharing purpose, encouraging growth, and bringing out the best in those around us.

The CCI Framework forms the foundation of relatability in all contexts. While my previous work explored this framework's application across personal, romantic, and professional relationships, this book narrows our focus to leadership in a multigenerational workforce. However, these principles remain universally applicable. If you master them in a leadership context, you can uplevel your connections in all areas of life.

We'll delve deep into what makes a leader genuinely relatable through proprietary research, extensive client work, and interviews with exemplary leaders. By the final page, you'll be equipped to apply these skills in any leadership scenario, from daily team interactions to global initiatives. The CCI Framework isn't just about becoming a better leader—it's about becoming a more relatable human being, capable of creating meaningful connections wherever you are.

THE RESEARCH

I am a research nerd. I've considered continuing my studies to have access to educational libraries. In my book, *relatable*, I prided myself on a research-backed approach to building connections, and this book will be no different. Okay, it will be somewhat different because, for *The Relatable Leader*, I've engaged in my own proprietary research to supplement interviews with top leaders and scores of peer-reviewed studies that support the principles within.

Intending to research the difference between what employees are seeking in leadership and how leaders are presenting themselves, I engaged in a study of 400 professionals in a variety of industries throughout the United States. Respondents were equally divided between Gen Z (eighteen to twenty-six years old), millennials (twenty-seven to forty-two), Gen X (forty-three to fifty-eight), and baby boomers (over fifty-nine). The study included 215 employees who supervised at least one other employee and 185 without direct reports. Respondents who supervised five or more direct reports were asked questions directed at leaders. The overall results have a margin of sampling error of plus or minus 5 percent at the .95 level of confidence.

If I were a betting woman (I am), I would have put everything on the findings that there was an enormous difference between the responses of employees versus leaders. I was sure that the disconnect was between what teams are looking for in their leadership (assuming vulnerability, self-awareness, and care) and how leaders thought they needed to act (motivated, inspirational, resilient). I was wrong. Don't tell my husband I've admitted to this.

We are far more aligned than I expected, but what surprised me the most was *what* employees were seeking from their leadership.

GENERATIONAL DIFFERENCES

Another element of surprise was the contrast between generations. Perhaps surprise is a strong word for something that has been repeatedly studied and classified, but it wasn't the fact that there *were* unexpected differences; it was how the differences manifested that was most interesting.

As mentioned above, the study had an equal number of respondents distributed through the generations. The distribution was done intentionally even though the current workforce breakdown, according to the US Census Bureau, is 5 percent Gen Z, 35 percent millennials, 33 percent Gen X, and 25 percent baby boomers. You may wonder why we would sample evenly with only 5 percent of the workforce being Gen Z. Still, in the upcoming years, younger workers will be a majority percentage of labor, with the Department of Labor estimating 64 percent will be millennials and Gen Z workers by 2030.

Workforce by Generation

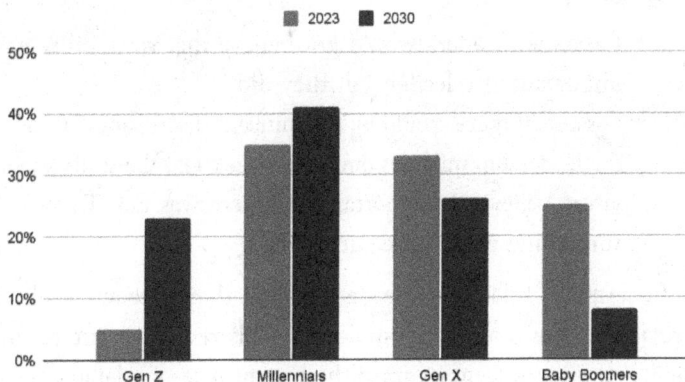

Note to readers—if you Google "millennials in the workforce 75 percent," you will encounter a bizarre phenomenon wherein thousands of sites (including several highly reputable ones) state that millennials will make up 75 percent of the workforce by 2025 or 2030 (apparently, the original source was unclear as to when the other generations would be annihilated).[1] This 75 percent figure is highly inaccurate. However, millennials will be the largest percentage at 41 percent, and understanding their psychology and needs should remain a focus.

Throughout this book, we will break down the generational differences in the data so that you, as a leader of a multi-generational workforce, can tailor your words and actions to benefit your teams and your goals the most.

---

1   Lettink, A. (2021, January 27). No, millennials will NOT be 75% of the workforce in 2025 (or ever)! LinkedIn. https://www.linkedin.com/pulse/millennials-75-workforce-2025-ever-anita-lettink

*"Assumptions are not barriers; they're bridges
to understanding waiting to be crossed."*

Let's dive into assumptions. My two main hypotheses were proven wrong:

- I assumed leaders would not believe that relatability was important as a leader, but they did.
- I assumed there would be a significant discrepancy between the leadership qualities employees seek and the traits supervisors believe are important, but there was not. There was something even more surprising.

In terms of relatability, leaders believe that a leader needs to be relatable even more than employees. This reveals an interesting insight—managers seem to grasp the significance of relatable leadership even more than their teams. They expect it from themselves.

It is important for a leader to be relatable:

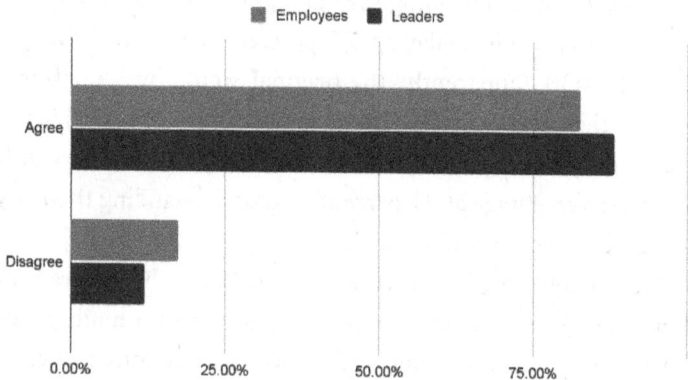

It is equally fascinating that while leaders believe relatability is important, they also recognize that most leaders are not putting this into practice. Over 40 percent of leaders surveyed put themselves in the outdated model of being "all-business, all the time." This gap between leaders understanding the value of relatability but simultaneously admitting they fall short is a key insight we will dive into in future chapters. Leaders are aware they should be showing their human side, yet a disconnect exists between their beliefs and actions.

The second hypothesis was that there would be significant disparities between the leadership qualities employees seek and the traits supervisors think they should demonstrate. I was again surprised—rather than gaps, there was alignment.

Yet, there *was* a disconnect.

The most significant divergence was between popular leadership discourse and what the research indicates. A quick Google search for the top qualities a leader should possess leads to quite a variety of attributes opined by experts and thought leaders. Before the study, I assumed authenticity, vulnerability, and care would be at the top—which is far more in line with the building blocks of most relationships. However, the survey data revealed that *leadership is different*. Employees and supervisors were asked to select the five top qualities for relatable leadership. The responses showed:

Employees	Leaders
1. Respectful	1. Respectful
2. Trustworthy	2. Trustworthy
3. Communicates Clearly	3. Caring
4. Active Listener	4. Communicates Clearly
5. Honest/Transparent	5. Motivated

"Respectful" and "trustworthy" topped the list.

The answer was the same for every generation, for all genders, employees, and leaders alike. (Of note, millennials rank trustworthy as number one, with respectful as a close second.) As I unpacked the data and corroborated the findings with peer-reviewed research and interviews, it made absolute sense.

It should also be noted that these traits *have* topped lists in the past, especially the need to be respected by a leader. Yet, in the past decade, there has been a shift toward prioritizing traits like vulnerability, compassion, and resilience—more transformational qualities. While these remain vital, the pendulum may have swung too far away from the basic foundations of leadership. We need to establish the fundamental building blocks of respect and trust before layering on elements such as vulnerability. What emerged here is a re-centering on the fundamentals of trust and respect that enable safety as a precursor to innovation, engagement, and collaboration.

CONNECTED, COMMUNICATIVE, INSPIRED LEADERS

As we unpack the pillars of relatable leadership from the data, current research studies, and professional experience, the foundational tenets of *relatable* remain intact—connect, communicate, inspire—and they are *all* infused with respect.

- *Connect*—how leaders can build trust through honesty, transparency, and authenticity.
- *Communicate*—where clear communication, active listening, and recognition foster understanding.
- *Inspire*—how purpose and motivation unleash potential.

Throughout *The Relatable Leader*, we will dive deeper into this blueprint, uncovering actionable insights and tools to evolve into the connected, communicative, inspired leader today's workforce is looking for. Here is a glimpse of what's to come:

Connect. Chapters 3 and 4. Your ability to create connections is at its highest when you lead in a way that invokes trustworthiness through your authenticity, transparency, and respect. We will unpack how to earn trust and develop psychological safety by showing your human side—imperfections and all.

Communicate. Chapters 5 and 6. We'll explore how clear, concise communication and active, empathetic listening make employees feel truly understood. We will also discuss how personalized recognition and understanding motivations inspire far more than public praise.

Inspire. Chapters 8 and 9. Connecting and communicating will set you apart, but then what? Inspiration takes leadership to the next level. It's time to unlock intrinsic motivation and purpose to fuel achievement. We're going to make you a beacon that draws out people's best without burning them out.

The final chapters will also address common hurdles you may encounter on the journey to relatable leadership—and how to overcome them with self-awareness and emotional intelligence.

The Relatable Leader will provide the roadmap you need to:

- Build trust and understanding to foster strong connections
- Enhance communication through recognition and clarity
- Unleash inspiration by empowering purpose and potential

And it all starts with respect.

CONNECTION CATALYSTS

What assumptions are you making about your team?

_____

_____

_____

_____

Where do you see evidence of a disconnect between what they need and how you are showing up?

_____

_____

_____

_____

CHAPTER 2

Respect: More than Words

Leila couldn't have been more excited to start her first official job. After four years of college, three internships, and large looming student loan payments, Leila was ecstatic to enter the "real world." She had landed a position as a digital marketing coordinator at a national residential home builder and was full of ideas, hope, and...a large dose of naïveté. After all, her corporate experience to date involved being wooed as an intern after being recruited from her college campus. It was a position where she was asked for little in terms of work product and given much in terms of perks—ping pong and pizza parties painted a bit of an inaccurate picture of what true day-to-day life would look like in her full-time position.

It was her first team meeting to discuss a new advertising campaign, and had ideas. As she slid into the last open chair and placed her notepad down on the conference table, she looked around at her colleagues, many of whom she hadn't been formally introduced to yet, and smiled—"I've made it," she thought to herself.

"Let's begin," Bill, the director of development, bellowed. A presentation filled the screen, and slide by slide, Sara's colleagues weighed in on copy, content, and visuals. Every time Leila raised her hand to speak, Bill gave her a terse shake of his head, indicating "not now," before moving on to comments from her more established colleagues. As the meeting concluded, Leila stayed back and confidently approached Bill with one idea that she was sure could make an impact. After all, the campaign was aimed at young renters, and as the only twenty-two-year-old on the team, no one else would have a similar finger on the pulse. "Hmm, no," Bill replied, and without further explanation, left the conference room and a dejected Leila behind.

It may have been the first meeting, but it would not be the last time Sara's voice was disregarded. A similar tone continued throughout the following months from both Bill and Sara's direct manager. Fed up, Leila asked for a meeting to discuss her ideas and her frustrations. "I've done extensive research into our new campaign, and I think our current position is missing the mark of our target demo. I also have to say it feels like I am not taken seriously here. I have some great ideas, but all I've been given is spreadsheets to organize them."

"Yet another entitled millennial," muttered Bill.

"I'm actually Gen Z," Leila replied.

Sadly, the meeting ended without much change. Sara's ideas remained shelved, and the company went on to launch a campaign that failed to excite their intended demographic. Over time, Leila became less and less interested in investing in her work. Her passion and confidence dwindled, and her resentment grew. The constant lack of respect and validation from her leaders led Leila to withdraw and do the bare minimum. The final straw was when Bill publicly criticized her for a minor mistake. Leila left the meeting in tears, resigning the following day, sadly causing a loss of fresh perspectives, innovative ideas, and the opportunity to begin to build a diverse, multigenerational team.

Sara's emotions ran the gamut during her employment, but the most palpable one? The feeling that she wasn't respected. Sara's experience isn't unique. In fact, it reflects a fundamental need in the workplace that often goes unmet. When I dove into the data, I was surprised by just how crucial respect proved to be.

In my research, respect from leadership didn't just make the list of desired traits for a relatable leader—it topped the charts. Nearly 60 percent of respondents ranked it as a necessary component. Respect beat out all the buzzworthy qualities like resilience, self-awareness, and even one of the most talked-about elements of modern leadership, vulnerability. Respect remained at the top even when the population was segmented—across genders, positions, and generations (though trust eked out over respect for millennials, it was still at the top).

Qualities of a Relatable Leader

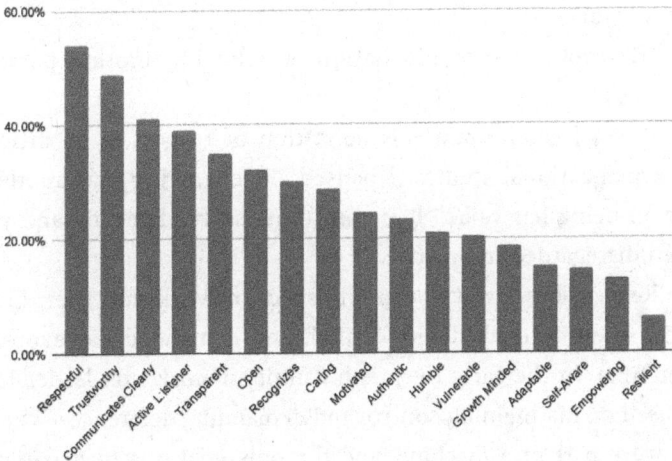

The results were surprising initially. Seemingly, much of the thought leadership surrounding leadership today focuses on traits like authenticity, vulnerability, and emotional intelligence. While these are clearly qualities leaders should aspire to have, the data shows that we are skipping steps. We cannot have authentic, vulnerable relationships with our teams without a proper foundation of respect.

WHAT IS RESPECT?

There are many definitions of respect, ranging from being treated politely to the absence of disrespect. Philosophers have also tackled the topic, offering their own perspectives. Kant's philosophical teachings could be extrapolated to define respect as well, wherein he believed that we should treat people as an end in themselves and not as a means to an end. The idea is that individuals have an inherent worth, regardless of their capabilities. Research involving the context of respect in the workplace abounds as well. However, the best definition I have found for respect in relation to our purposes is this:

"Respect is the manifestation of believing another person has value."

When I came upon this definition of respect in an article on organizational studies, I paused. "Recognizing that another human being has value." It is something so fundamental and yet often disregarded in practice.

Respect has always been an aspect of work; however, how it has been defined, demonstrated, and demanded has evolved over time. In the early twentieth century, theories on leadership focused on maintaining control and demanding deference—workers were part of a machine, and the only goal was to maximize productivity. There was a distinct hierarchy and top-down control. Respect was a key component of leadership, but the focus was on the respect leaders demanded, without consideration for the respect of the employee.

Much of this shifted post-World War II and during the social movements of the sixties and seventies. The economy was far more stable, which allowed self-expression and individual contributions to take center stage—employees began seeking a better quality of life. With work–life balance and career satisfaction becoming a priority, organizations began to recognize that they needed to adapt their culture and practices.

This shift in workplace dynamics paved the way for a new approach to respect at work. The concept of mutual respect—between leaders and employees, as well as among coworkers—began to gain traction. Organizations began to recognize that nurturing a culture of respect at all levels could lead to increased engagement, innovation, and, ultimately, better business ROI. While this book and the research that supports it focuses on respect *from* leadership, mutual respect is the ideal—and a likely outcome when the former is a part of the culture. Mutual respect between leaders and teams has been found to raise job satisfaction and improve engagement. Employees who feel respected feel encouraged and supported, and they feel far more connected to the success of their organization. They are more invested in collaboration and are better, more positive communicators within their team. In spite of research consistently demonstrating the advantages of respectful leadership, it still fails to be practiced in a large percentage of organizations.

ALWAYS IN FASHION

As I expressed earlier, I was shocked when respect topped the list in my research. It seemed almost...old school. The rhetoric around leadership has us focusing on baring our souls, admitting our failures, and showing up as our whole selves. These are all absolutely valuable traits of a great leader. However, in our rush to dive deeper and find some new secret sauce, it's as if we have forgotten the basics. We've been so focused on building the penthouse that we've forgotten to finish the foundation.

The truth is that past research has included respect as a key leadership trait, but we've allowed it to be ignored in exchange for more exciting concepts. Respect never really went out of style; we just stopped paying attention to it. A 2009 study found that employees ranked working for someone who treats them with respect over autonomy, purpose, job security, and income. A 2008 study demonstrated organizational respect significantly reduced emotional exhaustion among employees and improved well-being. A 2016 survey by the Society for Human Resource Management ranked respectful treatment at work as the most important factor boosting job satisfaction.

It's a clear picture. Respect isn't a fleeting, nice-to-have idea; it's fundamental. While several traits encompass a great, relatable leader, respect is the foundation of it all. As leaders, we need to recalibrate our focus. We can strike a balance between embracing the new concepts of leadership with the timeless principle of believing everyone as if they have value—because they do. As we move forward in our exploration of relatable leadership, let's keep this fundamental truth at the forefront of our minds: Respect is the foundation upon which all other aspects of effective leadership are built.

But here's the million (billion?)-dollar question: If respect is so timeless, why does it feel like we're rediscovering just how important it is? The answer lies in the ever-changing landscape of our multi-generational workforce.

GENERATIONAL DISRESPECT

What if the refocus on respect was a response to generational disrespect? Many employees, especially millennials and Gen Z, feel they're not receiving the respect they deserve. Remember Sara? Unfortunately, the accusations of laziness, entitlement, and selfishness that are often hurled at younger generations serve only to widen the disconnect between leaders and their teams. Born from a cocktail of assumptions and misunderstandings, this lack of respect creates barriers that undermine the very foundations of a connected, engaged workforce.

Take millennials, for instance. Despite being recognized as collaborative, tech-savvy, and efficient multitaskers, they're repeatedly characterized as fragile, needy, and demanding. The kicker? These stereotypes are often based on sample sizes of one individual's opinions. It's as if we are trying to see the worst in a generation that's reshaping the workplace landscape, lest we forget that millennials will make up the largest percentage of the workforce by 2030 at 41 percent.

Gen Z faces similar criticism, where the desire for work–life balance is perceived as lazy, and their mental health challenges abound. Of note, Gen Z was the first generation born into immersive social media, national tragedy, and a world of constant connectivity. They've grown up with smartphones permanently in their hands from adolescence on and have navigated a digital landscape no other generation has experienced.

This is not to say that Gen X and the baby boomers have escaped divisive stereotypes. Gen X, "the forgotten generation," is often dubbed cynical, independent, and less likely to be loyal to a job. These perceptions may stem from growing up during times of increasing divorce rates and economic uncertainty and being raised by workaholic boomer parents—the rise of the latchkey kids. Gen X is also the first generation to grow up with personal computers, with the internet arriving in adulthood, requiring a complete pivot toward foreign technology.

Boomers? They are categorized as resistant to change and technologically inept. Sure, my mom still has a flip phone, but I can assure you there are plenty of boomers who are breaking that stereotype. They are a diverse group with a wide range of skills and knowledge. They also have one of the strongest work ethics around them.

The problem is, these labels aren't just unfair; they're destructive. In many cases, hints of truth are backed by justification—perhaps Gen Z struggles more openly with mental health, but what generation has been made more aware of mental well-being? These stereotypes blind us to the unique strengths and perspectives each generation brings to the table. They destroy the potential for collaboration and engagement and create self-fulfilling prophecies where those who are constantly battling against these perceptions start to disengage or live down to the low expectations set for them.

With all this in mind, it's no wonder that respect emerged as the most critical trait desired in leadership. Respect transcends generational divides. It eradicates stereotypes and misconceptions. Respect breaks down barriers and creates a foundation where authentic relationships can be built and collaboration across generations can occur.

Can you imagine a world in which every leader believed *every* team member had value regardless of stereotypes and projections?

Where the potential and worth of every employee was recognized? The story of Leila being undervalued and dismissed is echoed throughout the workplace, but it doesn't have to be.

People need to feel that they matter. When we respect someone, we see them as having inherent worth, regardless of their age, experience, or position. We value their perspectives and ideas, and we create space for them to contribute. By showing respect, we build trust, foster collaboration, and unlock the full potential of every individual on our team.

Imagine if Bill had taken a different approach—one rooted in respect for Sara's potential and perspectives. What if, instead of dismissing her and her ideas outright simply based on her youth, he had taken the time to listen, understand, and provide constructive feedback? The outcome could have been markedly different.

HOW CAN LEADERS SHOW RESPECT?

Now that we've discussed what respect is, where it is lacking, and why it's necessary, it's time to delve into the practical application. How can leaders translate the concept of respect into tangible actions that their teams will acknowledge and recognize? In this section, we will explore actionable tips and concrete strategies that leaders can use to create a culture of respect. Remember, above all, respect is a state of mind and a state of being, and oftentimes created through daily interactions and small consistent actions. Here are three actionable strategies:

Respectful leaders actively listen and get curious

Respectful leadership is fundamentally rooted in effective communication, particularly through active listening and, my favorite, curious listening. Research has shown that leaders and managers spend a significant portion of their time, between 70 percent and 90 percent, communicating, and yet employees consistently rate communication from their leaders poorly. Actively listening to your teams and going one step further to ask curious questions is essential to building a culture of respect. The research supports this, finding that asking questions and attentively listening are hallmarks of respectful leadership.

However, this is more than just being polite. Actively listening means you are fully engaged in the conversation and interacting thoughtfully. Try the EARS method to remember the main points of actively listening during a conversation:

E—Engage fully with your complete attention focused
A—Ask questions to show curiosity and improve understanding.
R—Reflect back main points by paraphrasing or summarizing.
S—Suspend judgment and avoid interrupting.

Curiosity is simply the next level of active listening, the A in EARS. By asking open-ended questions and focusing on learning as opposed to leading, you create an environment where team members feel heard, valued, and important. Active listening and curiosity demonstrate respect for your team's thoughts and ideas and cultivate an environment that supports open (and more efficient) communication.

Respectful leaders are considerate

Consideration is a form of respect that centers on being mindful of someone's feelings, needs, and environment. "Consideration is the degree to which a leader shows concern and respect for followers, looks out for their welfare, and expresses appreciation and support." A considerate leader improves employee job satisfaction, effectiveness, and motivation. In some ways, consideration draws on active listening and curiosity as it requires leaders to take the time to actually understand their team members, their circumstances, and their challenges. Leaders who are considerate make an effort to acclimate to their team's needs—including their culture, abilities, and family status. Leaders who are considerate also take into account the impact of their words and actions on their teams.

A respectful leader focusing on being more considerate would ask questions like:

"How are you doing today?"
"Is there anything you need help with?"
"What challenges are you facing in your work right now?"
"How can I better support you in your role?"

By demonstrating consideration through these types of questions and paying attention to employee needs, leaders create an environment of respect.

Respectful leaders are fair and equitable

Fair leaders "build better relationships with their followers, engender more positive attitudes and emotions, and seem able to engender more desirable and less undesirable behavior."

A fair leader applies the same standards to all team members. They avoid personal projections and biases. They make decisions based on merit and objective criteria. They provide criticism constructively and equitably. With a fair leader, teams are confident their efforts are valued. This trust leads them to be far more receptive to feedback and, ultimately, become a more engaged and productive team.

Remember, *respect is the manifestation that another human being has value.* Giving someone the power of your attention, being considerate, and being fair and equitable are all ways to show that you recognize their inherent worth.

BUILD A BASELINE

How can we be sure that our teams are being shown respect from leadership? We ask. Former senior vice president of People Operations at Google, Laszlo Bock, shared in a 2013 *New York Times* interview that "we've actually made it harder to be a bad manager." Each year, even after Bock left Google in 2017, employees are given the Googlegeist survey, asking questions regarding engagement, values, compensation, and their managers. One of the areas frequently included? Whether leaders treat their team with respect. Bock states, "These are fundamental things that turn out to be really important in making people feel excited and happy and wanting to go the extra mile for you." The results are then used to identify areas *and* leaders that are in need of improvement. It also creates a way to hold leaders accountable. If they have a manager consistently getting lower scores, for example, they work to change the results. It creates a culture where respect is valued, where it is measurable and actionable. The employees know that the survey is intended to go beyond checking the pulse; it's meant to create change. Google is not alone in frequently surveying their teams; many organizations consistently tap into their greatest source of information—their teams.

"Don't ask the question if you aren't prepared to hear the answer," or its various iterations, is a popular saying of unknown origin, and this mindset often results in leaders and organizations failing to ask the right questions out of fear that the answers will require effort. It reminds me of one of my former consulting clients. They were in the midst of a merger, with teammates, leaders, and values from two very different organizations attempting to come together. Tensions were high and morale was low. I recommended we survey the team to get a baseline for growth and learn from negative feedback. The powers that be refused, stating it would "open a can of worms." They were convinced it would exacerbate an already stressful situation.

It was a critical mistake. The team felt as if their frustrations were irrelevant and their voices unheard, growing resentment and unrest. Leadership made assumptions and decisions with little more than guesswork, and the integration process was painful. Productivity slowed, and turnover was through the roof, including key talent that ended up costing the organization hundreds of thousands to replace and retrain. Their failure to be willing to ask hard questions and work toward addressing challenges was far more expensive than they realized.

How can you ask the questions that matter? How can you ensure that your leadership is held accountable? More specifically, for this chapter, how can we ensure that respect remains at the forefront of your organizational culture? We may as well ask the questions—even if the answer is stressful, painful, or expensive—because if we allow issues to fester and go unchecked, all they do is become MORE stressful, MORE painful, and WAY MORE expensive. Seek out the truth and utilize that information to meet your teams where they are.

What if you don't have the systems and processes to implement a traditional employee engagement survey? Truthfully, you don't need to; you can create a survey online (Google Forms, SurveyMonkey, Jotform) and ask a few questions in a way that allows your employees to remain anonymous and provide candid feedback (spoiler alert: I've included an example survey you can deploy at the end of this book.). In each chapter, I will include suggested questions you can ask to gauge how well you and your organization are embodying the trait of that chapter. You can use some or all of them, depending on your company's goals and generational makeup.

Remember, the goal isn't just to ask questions but to create an environment where employees feel heard and leaders are held accountable. Actions based on insights are how we will build a more collaborative and invested workforce. Of note, I prefer to use a four-point Likert scale utilizing statements ranging from Completely Disagree to Completely Agree for a more nuanced insight, such as:

	COMPLETELY DISAGREE	DISAGREE	AGREE	COMPLETELY AGREE
I feel respected by my immediate supervisor.				
I feel my ideas and contributions are valued.				
I feel comfortable expressing my opinions, even if they are different from my leaders.				
I believe leadership treats all team members equally and fairly.				
In meetings and discussions, all team members have the opportunity to be heard.				

Choose the statements that align most with your goals, mix and match throughout the ones offered in this book, and create a survey that will allow your teams to feel seen and heard. The real test of leadership is in how the responses are acknowledged, addressed, and acted upon.

FINAL THOUGHTS

Respect transcends generational divides and stems from the innate human desire to feel valued. Recognizing the inherent worth of every individual on your team and their contributions will do more for your organization's success, employee engagement, and bottom line than any buzzworthy trend. In a world where change is constant, respect is timeless.

CONNECTION CATALYSTS

How do you actively demonstrate respect to team members?

_____
_____
_____
_____

What assumptions or stereotypes might you be holding about different generations in your workplace? How can you challenge these assumptions to create a more respectful environment?

_____
_____
_____
_____

In what ways can you create more opportunities for all team members, regardless of age or experience, to contribute their ideas and perspectives?

_____

_____

_____

_____

PART ONE

CONNECT

CHAPTER 3

Trust: The Path to Psychological Safety

"Give safety, get innovation."

Imagine this: a team meeting where ideas are shared freely, an open-door policy where employees can bring a mistake to their manager, allowing for a quicker resolution, a company town hall where employees share suggestions for improving processes, and a performance review where constructive criticism is focused on growth and well received. This isn't a utopian fantasy; this is what happens when trust is prioritized.

Trust is not a luxury—it's the foundation upon which all meaningful connections, collaborations, and innovations are built. It's also at the top of the list of what makes a relatable leader across all generations. In fact, across all age groups, genders, and roles, trust consistently ranked in the top three qualities of relatable leaders in my research. Of note is that trust was ranked as the number one most important quality in a leader for both millennials and boomers, just above respect. This cross-generational focus on trust shows just how essential it is in today's workplace. For leaders hoping to engage their teams, actively building and maintaining trust is non-negotiable—it's been found to increase job performance, job satisfaction, and organizational commitment.[1]

Unfortunately, there's an enormous gap between the desire of today's workforce for trustworthy leaders and the reality of many organizations. According to Gallup, only 21 percent of employees in the US strongly agree that they trust the leadership within their organization.[2] This trust deficit has serious consequences for engagement, retention, and overall organizational success.

COGNITIVE VS. AFFECTIVE TRUST

Organizational research has identified two primary categories of trust that shape our professional relationships: cognitive trust and affective trust.[3] They are different but very much interrelated—both necessary for optimal team dynamics.

Cognitive trust is the rational, logic-based belief in someone's competence, honesty, and dependability.[4] It's built through consistency, follow-through on commitments, and proven competence.

Affective trust is an emotional bond based on genuine care, empathy, and concern for one's well-being.[5] Affective trust devel-

---

1 Dirks, K. T., & Ferrin, D. L. (2002). Trust in leadership: Meta-analytic findings and implications for research and practice. *Journal of Applied Psychology, 87*(4), 611–628. https://doi.org/10.1037/0021-9010.87.4.611

2 McLain, D., & Pendell, R. (2023). Why trust in leaders is faltering and how to gain it back. *Gallup.* https://www.gallup.com/workplace/473738/why-trust-leaders-faltering-gain-back.aspx

3 Baer, M. D., Frank, E. L., Matta, F. K., Luciano, M. M., & Wellman, N. (2021). Undertrusted, overtrusted, or just right? The fairness of (in)congruence between trust wanted and trust received. *Academy of Management Journal, 64*(1), 180–206. https://doi.org/10.5465/amj.2018.0334

4 Dirks & Ferrin, 2002.

5 McAllister, D. J. (1995). Affect- and cognition-based trust as foundations for interpersonal cooperation in organizations. *Academy of Management Journal, 38*(1), 24–59. https://www.jstor.org/stable/256727

ops through compassion and showing a real interest in employees as individuals.

Both types of trust are important, but affective trust is what builds stronger, more resilient teams. Ultimately, while cognitive trust allows employees to believe in their leader's abilities and competence, affective trust creates a truly committed team. When employees feel their leaders genuinely care about them as people, not just as human capital (a term that needs to be removed from our vernacular), they work harder, remain engaged, and are far more likely to go above and beyond.

Sofia had been working as an associate at her law firm for just over a year. She was just starting to find her flow and take on more responsibility when she received devastating news—her father had suffered a severe stroke. Sofia's mom had passed away when she was just a young girl, and it had been Sofia and her dad as an unbreakable duo for the majority of her life. Sofia was distraught—both with worry for her father's health and the prospect of asking her boss for time off work.

Sofia's hands trembled as she knocked on Monique's door. "Come in," Monique called out. Sofia inhaled deeply and shared, "Monique, I have a personal matter that I need to talk to you about." Fighting back tears, Sofia shared the news of her father's condition and the fact that she was his only family and sole caregiver.

Monique's expression softened. She said, "I'm so sorry to hear about your dad; a stroke can be so sudden and debilitating. Please, tell me how I can help." Sofia felt the tension begin to leave her body, surprised and relieved by Monique's kindness. She shared her desire to help arrange her father's care and to be with him during these initial stages. "I can absolutely do much of my work remotely—I know that my caseload is heavy right now, but there will be a lot of downtime during his therapy appointments."

"Of course, Sofia. Family comes first. We'll make this work," Monique replied. "Take the time you need. We will get you set up to work from home and cover any in-person appearances. Just focus on your father right now." Monique then shared that her own grandfather had suffered a stroke three years ago, and she understood the road to recovery they were facing. "My door is always open," she added.

In the months that followed, Monique regularly checked in on Sofia—making sure her workload was manageable and offering support. It was a slow and difficult path, but Sofia's dad eventually made a full recovery. Sofia would forever be grateful for the time, support, and care she was afforded from her work.

Years later, when Sofia became a partner, she never forgot Monique's kindness and always endeavored to emulate that same level of empathy and support for her own team members. She recognized that Monique's leadership and care not only helped her during one of the most difficult times in her life but also shaped her as a leader and cemented her commitment to the firm.

The story of Sofia and Monique illustrates how affective trust, built through genuine care and empathy, can profoundly impact an employee's experience, loyalty, and commitment to an organization. As leaders, developing both cognitive and affective trust—but especially effective—creates a workplace where team members feel valued. Competence and compassion cultivate environments where trust thrives, ultimately leading to better collaboration and productivity.

TRUST AND PSYCHOLOGICAL SAFETY

Creating a high-trust work culture sets the stage for success, but it also paves the way for another essential aspect of workplace dynamics: psychological safety. Trust and psychological safety are closely connected, with trust laying the foundation for a psychologically safe workplace.

Trust, as we've explored, is the foundation of interpersonal relationships in the workplace between leaders and teams and within teams themselves. Trust allows team members to rely on each other and their intentions. Psychological safety, on the other hand, goes beyond person-to-person relationships and involves the team as a whole.

Psychological safety, a concept established nearly seventy-five years ago, is defined as when employees feel comfortable being themselves at work.[6] Research suggests that psychological safety allows self-expression and risk-taking without fear of judgment or rejection.[7] Creating a psychologically safe environment increases innovation, collaboration, and improves team attitudes and performance.[8] When employees trust their leaders and feel psychologically safe, they're more likely to speak up with new ideas, admit mistakes, take risks, and engage in healthy debate.

6   Kahn, W. A. (1990). Psychological conditions of personal engagement and disengagement at work. *Academy of Management Journal, 33*(4), 692–724. https://www.jstor.org/stable/256287

7   Kim, S., Lee, H., & Connerton, T. P. (2020). How psychological safety affects team performance: Mediating role of efficacy and learning behavior. *Frontiers in Psychology, 11.* https://doi.org/10.3389/fpsyg.2020.01581

8   Edmondson, A. C., & Lei, Z. (2014). Psychological safety: The history, renaissance, and future of an interpersonal construct. *Annual Review of Organizational Psychology and Organizational Behavior, 1,* 23–43. https://doi.org/10.1146/annurev-orgpsych-031413-091305

Trust creates the setting for psychological safety, which then unlocks the full potential of teams. Here are five ways to create a psychologically safe environment built on a foundation of trust:

1. Encourage open communication. Cultivate a culture where team members feel comfortable speaking up, even when their opinions and ideas counter the status quo.

2. Normalize learning from mistakes. Being able to learn from failures is both a result of a psychologically safe environment *and* contributes to creating one.

3. Promote inclusion. Ensure team members of all ranks have an opportunity to contribute and actively seek diverse opinions and perspectives.

4. Establish clear boundaries. A psychologically safe workplace has clear guidelines for what is acceptable behavior.

5. Be the example. As a leader, it's not just okay but also imperative to admit when you don't have all the answers and share your own humanity; your authenticity will lead the way (we'll get into that more in the next chapter).

By understanding the link between trust and psychological safety, leaders can encourage an atmosphere where team members feel empowered to bring their full selves to work, take calculated risks, and drive innovation.

HOW TO BUILD TRUST—THE FOUR CS

We now know that building trust as a leader is fundamental and critical to the success of an organization, but how is trust built? The concept of trust can seem abstract, but research has identified several key ways to build trust as a leader. I call them "The Four Cs" of trustworthy leadership. These four essential components provide a practical framework for leaders looking to strengthen trust within their teams and organizations.

Communication

Open, clear communication is the foundation of trust.[9] We will explore communication as a leader in greater detail in Chapter 5, but we also need to highlight the elements that are necessary to build a trusting relationship. What does open, clear communication entail? Leaders who communicate clearly and honestly. They share information even when it's difficult. They explain the reasons behind their decisions. They're willing to have tough conversations. While all these contribute to being a trustworthy leader and communicator, one of the most vital ways in which leaders communicate is when they are willing to admit they don't have all the answers and that they, too, make mistakes. My study revealed an interesting disconnect between the perceptions of employees and leaders. While employees believed that leaders who shared their mistakes made them more trustworthy, the leaders disagreed. This suggests that supervisors may be underestimating the power of vulnerability in relation to their imperfections.

Competence

Competence is the second pillar needed to build trust between a leader in their team.[10] Competence encompasses the skills and knowledge related to the leader's role and duties, including deci-

---

9   Clapp-Smith, R., Vogelgesang, G. R., & Avey, J. B. (2009). Authentic leadership and positive psychological capital: The mediating role of trust at the group level of analysis. *Journal of Leadership & Organizational Studies, 15*(3), 227–240. https://doi.org/10.1177/1548051808326596

10 Byun, G., Dai, Y., Lee, S., & Kang, S. (2017). Leader trust, competence, LMX, and member performance: A moderated mediation framework. *Psychological Reports, 120*(6), 1137–1159. https://doi.org/10.1177/003329 4117716465

sion-making, problem-solving, and their ability to guide their team toward goals. When employees feel that their leader is competent, they are more inclined to follow their direction and trust their judgment.

Employees need to trust that their leaders know what they're doing. Competent leaders have extensive knowledge in the areas necessary, but they are always learning, they make decisions that are based on logic and experience, and they tackle challenges head-on. We need to recognize that competence isn't about knowing everything but having the wherewithal to find solutions and make good decisions.

Consistency

The third element required to build trust as a leader is consistency, through their words and actions.[11] Do they follow through on what they say and what they commit to? This is not dissimilar to building trust in any relationship. Consistency in leadership means they are reliable and predictable in behavior, decision-making, and communication. When leaders are consistent, team members know what to expect and feel more secure in their work environment.

Consistent leaders follow through on commitments and promises, apply rules fairly and equitably, and they walk the talk, aligning words with actions. On the other hand, when leaders are inconsistent, it can lead to confusion, anxiety, and a lack of trust among team members.

---

11 Iqbal, S., Farid, T., Khan, M. K., Zhang, Q., Khattak, A., & Ma, J. (2019). Bridging the Gap between Authentic Leadership and Employees Communal Relationships through Trust. *International Journal of Environmental Research and Public Health, 17*(1), 250. https://doi.org/10.3390/ijerph17010250

Dr. Chen experienced this firsthand. When she first joined the hospital's pediatric department, she could not have been more excited until she experienced her supervisor's leadership style. One week, he would be championing innovative patient care and thinking "outside of the box," and the next, he'd chastise the team for not adhering strictly to established protocols. He'd wax poetic about work–life balance in staff meetings, only to demand overtime without notice. In team discussions, he'd encourage open dialogue but would then quickly shut down or dismiss ideas that didn't align with his own views. Any attempt to discuss these inconsistencies was rebuked. Dr. Chen found it nearly impossible to trust his directives or rely on his support, and neither could the rest of her team.

Dr. Chen's experience is a compelling reminder of how consistency is paramount in establishing trust in leadership. Consistent leadership builds a foundation of trust, allowing team members to focus on their work with confidence in their leader, leading to increased productivity, better team morale, and a more positive work culture overall.

Care

The fourth and final element essential to building trust as a leader is care. "Where people feel cared for, they are more likely to trust the carer."[12] A caring leader has genuine concern and empathy for their team members, their well-being, and their professional growth. When leaders care, they show empathy during difficult times and celebrate successes. It doesn't mean that boundaries

---

12 Louis, K. S., & Murphy, J. (2017). Trust, caring and organizational learning: The leader's role. *Journal of Educational Administration, 55*(1), 103–126. https://doi.org/10.1108/jea-07-2016-0077

are crossed or the leader has to develop an overly personal relationship but instead shows an authentic interest in their team as a human being.

Research has consistently shown that when employees feel cared for by their leaders, they are more likely to be engaged, loyal, and productive. According to Gallup, "your manager cares" is now one of the top five drivers of employee engagement.[13] When leaders show that they authentically care, it creates an environment where team members feel valued and understood, leading to increased trust and engagement.

REPAIRING BROKEN TRUST

I had just finished my keynote at an all-hands meeting for a large manufacturing company and was about to enter one of the most rewarding stages as a professional speaker—engaging face-to-face with audience members. Learning about what resonated, answering questions, and hearing personal stories bring the concepts I speak about to life through real-world scenarios. One of the first to step up was Eric, an emerging leader in his late thirties. "I'm so glad you talked about trust," Eric said. "I didn't think I was going to be here for this meeting. I thought I was going to have to quit."

Eric went on to explain that he was beyond excited to land what he considered to be his dream job. He was excited about the position, the company, and the potential for growth. Eric had been hired by a leader he initially found to be intelligent and charismatic, and he was eager to learn from his mentorship. Everything seemed perfect at first.

---

13 Gallup, Inc. (2024, July 22). How to improve employee engagement in the workplace. *Gallup.* https://www.gallup.com/workplace/285674/improve-employee-engagement-workplace.aspx#ite-357473

The situation was far from perfect. Eric learned that his manager, his mentor, was taking Eric's ideas and presenting them to clients and his higher-ups as his own. "I was beyond frustrated, and honestly, I had no idea what to do. This guy had been at the company for nearly a decade, and here I am, the new guy with quite a bombshell to drop. I wasn't sure anyone would believe me if I told them," Eric shared.

With his enthusiasm for his job rapidly dwindling, Eric hit a breaking point when his boss blamed him for a problem he hadn't created. "I couldn't keep quiet any longer; he was affecting my professional reputation." While he was worried about repercussions, he knew he needed to set the record straight and defend himself.

Eric gathered his evidence and requested a meeting with upper management where he shared the going-ons of the past months. Thankfully, his supervisor's managers recognized what was happening and took immediate action. Eric's contributions were recognized, and the leader was replaced. The actions of leadership allowed Eric to stay with the company, but the experience left a mark.

Eric's story reminds us of how quickly trust can be broken and how damaging it can be to productivity. When trust is broken, as in Eric's case, it can lead to valuable employees considering leaving, even when it is a position they once considered their dream job. On the other hand, when organizations actively work to repair broken trust, relationships and talent can be saved.

Every interaction is an opportunity to either strengthen or erode trust. Relatable leaders understand this and approach each day knowing that trust is the foundation upon which all other aspects of successful leadership are built. As we've seen, when you give safety through trust, you get innovation, engagement, and results in return.

THE IMPORTANCE OF MUTUAL TRUST

While the majority of this chapter has remained focused on building trust as a leader, we cannot ignore the importance of mutual trust and the trust that a leader has in their team. My research indicates that a trustworthy leader is a fundamental requirement of a relatable leader. However, research also highlights the importance of a leader trusting their employee.

Mutual trust at work isn't just about leaders earning the trust of their employees; it's also about leaders showing that they trust their employees. That they have confidence in their employee's ability to do their jobs without micromanagement and constant critique. A two-way street of trust is an unstoppable force, though at times a bit more difficult to navigate with the rise of remote and hybrid work.

I conducted an informal social media survey asking people what made a boss they had exceptional. The replies were eye-opening, and many emphasized the importance of feeling trusted by their leaders. Here is a sampling of the responses:

> "Flexible, *trusted me* and my knowledge, had empathy and compassion for my life outside of work."

> "Challenged me, *trusted me*, sincerely sought my position/ insight on situations and strategies."

> "*Trusts me* to do my job the way I need it to work for me."

> "*Trusted me* to do my job."

> "She *trusts me*, and I know she has my back if things go sideways."

> "Trusts me to do my job."

> "Truly respected and *trusted me*. Valued my input."

They trust me. What a powerful statement that underscores such an important aspect of leadership—believing in the team that you've created. When leaders show that they trust their employees, there is an increase in engagement, employee satisfaction, motivation, and commitment.[14]

Trust is not blind faith—trust is earned. The formula for building trust as an employee is the same foundational principles, whether it's an employee earning their manager's trust or a leader gaining the trust of their team. In order to earn trust, the employee is:

Communicative: Maintaining open and honest communication with their manager

Consistent: Reliably delivering on promises and meeting expectations

Competent: Demonstrating the skills and knowledge needed for their role

Caring: Showing genuine investment in the organization's success

These four Cs form the foundation of trust-building, and when leaders and employees have a mutual trusting relationship, it creates a positive feedback loop that with a multitude of positive effects. What happens when you find yourself struggling to trust your team? It's worth taking a moment to reflect. Is one of the four Cs missing? Are they communicative enough? Are they consistent in their deliverables? Do they show competence? Are

14 Cho, J., Schilpzand, P., Huang, L., & Paterson, T. (2020). How and when humble leadership facilitates employee job performance: The roles of feeling trusted and job autonomy. *Journal of Leadership & Organizational Studies*, 28(2), 169–184. https://doi.org/10.1177/1548051820979634

they showing that they care? Or is it something within you that may need to be addressed? Is it time to let go of control?

It should be noted that even when you do trust your team, the best leaders balance trust with appropriate levels of oversight, providing guidance and support as needed. In practice, leaders can show they trust their teams in a variety of ways, including:

- Allowing flexibility in how work is accomplished
- Seeking and valuing employee input in decision-making processes
- Avoiding micromanagement
- Providing opportunities for growth and development
- Supporting employees' ideas and initiatives

Cultivating mutual trust in the workplace, especially as we navigate the evolving landscape of work, including remote and hybrid models, maintaining and strengthening trust becomes even more of a priority. By prioritizing mutual trust, organizations can create high-performing teams ready to take on the next challenge.

FINAL THOUGHTS

Trust is like a WiFi signal—the stronger it is, the better the connection. Cultivating trust as a leader is more critical than ever and can drive engagement across generations. Remember, trust is a two-way street, and while being a trustworthy leader is vital, mutual trust between leaders and their teams is equally important. As you move forward in your leadership journey, prioritize building and maintaining trust through every interaction. Doing so will allow your team to feel valued, empowered, and resilient amongst challenges. In return? You'll receive a dedicated, motivated, and loyal team. That sounds like a solid exchange, in my opinion!

CONNECTION CATALYSTS

Reflect on a time when a leader's actions either significantly built or eroded your trust. What were the specific behaviors that led to that situation?

_____

_____

_____

_____

What is one concrete step you can take this week to actively build trust with your team?

_____

_____

_____

_____

How might you create more psychological safety in your next team meeting or one-on-one?

_____

_____

_____

_____

PART TWO

COMMUNICATE

CHAPTER 4

Authenticity: Daring to be Human

"The future belongs to leaders who dare to be human."

Employees began to pour into the flex area at headquarters, taking up the couches, pulling up chairs, and finding columns to lean against with their coffees. IT milled around, working to make sure those working from home could see and hear the podium. "Test, test, test—give a thumbs up if you can hear me," they said to the video wall of faces.

Darius, the CEO of a large technology company, called the meeting in response to a sudden market downturn affecting their industry. As he stepped up to the podium, a hush fell over the room.

"Thank you all for joining on such short notice," Darius began, his voice steady and calm. "I'm sure many of you have seen the news about the market shift we're facing. I want to address this head-on and share our plan moving forward."

For the next half hour, Darius laid out the facts of the situation. He didn't sugarcoat the challenges, nor did he catastrophize the situation. After explaining the challenges ahead, Darius outlined his plan to move forward.

As he neared the end of his talk, Darius paused, taking a sip of water. "I want to share something with you all," he said, his tone steady. "This isn't the first time I have experienced a situation like this. In my first role as a leader, I went through a similar market shift." Darius continued, "I remember how I felt—overwhelmed and, if I'm being honest, nervous for what's next. But what I learned then, and what I know now, is that these moments are opportunities for innovation and growth. We came out of that crisis stronger, and I'm confident we'll do the same here."

As Darius opened the floor for questions, a young product manager raised his hand. "How can you be so sure we'll make it through this?" he asked, his voice laced with anxiety.

Darius nodded, "It's a fair question, and the truth is, there are no guarantees. But what I am sure of is there is an incredible amount of talent and resilience in this room and on these screens. We have the skills and the determination to adapt. I've seen what this team can do, and I'm 100 percent confident we will weather this."

Nods of agreement rippled through the audience. Darius continued to field questions, balancing honesty and transparency about the challenges ahead with a clear confidence in the team's ability to overcome them.

As the town hall ended, there was a palpable shift in the energy of the room. The anxiety was still there, but it was tempered by the team's determination. Darius was both authentic and honest in his communication, but also inspiring and confident in his plan to overcome the challenges ahead. That meeting turned into a rallying point for the company.

There is power in authenticity in leadership. Darius didn't pretend to have the answers or be without concern, but he shared his personal experience with challenging times, which allowed him to connect with his team on a human level.

Authenticity has emerged as an essential element of leadership. As we explore the concept of becoming a relatable leader, we'll discover how being real and genuine is a necessary component in building a foundation for meaningful connections and engagement across teams. This chapter will explore what authenticity means in the context of leadership, how it affects organizations, and how you can integrate it into your leadership.

But what exactly do we mean by "authenticity" in a leadership context? Let's dive in.

AUTHENTICITY DEFINED

The most inspiring, relatable leaders bring their whole selves to their roles—imperfections and all. They are real, and they are authentic. I realize that "authenticity" has become quite the buzzword and may have lost some of its shine, but what it represents at its core still remains the cornerstone of connection. Authenticity can generally be described as alignment between *who someone is* and *how they present themselves* in the world.[1] *Cambridge Dictionary* defines it as "the quality of being real or true."[2]

When we apply the concept of authenticity to leadership, it takes on even greater significance. It isn't about being real and sharing your obsession with garden gnomes or your irrational fear of rubber bands (okay, that one's mine); it's about aligning your actions with your values.

---

1   Harter, S. (2002). Authenticity. In C. R. Snyder & S. J. Lopez (Eds.), *Handbook of Positive Psychology* (pp. 382–394). UK: Oxford University Press.

2   Authenticity. (2024). https://dictionary.cambridge.org/us/dictionary/english/authenticity

Many scholars define authentic leadership through four primary factors established in a 2007 study by Fred Walumbwa and his colleagues. The elements include:

1. Self-awareness: Knowing one's strengths, weaknesses, motives, and emotions

2. Relational transparency: Openly sharing thoughts and feelings

3. Balanced processing: Evaluating all facts before making a decision

4. Internalized moral perspective: Using an internal moral compass to guide decisions.[3]

These four research-based components provide a framework that creates a leadership style that is genuine, ethical, and effective. They bridge the gap between being authentic personally and being authentic as a leader, and show how your individuality can translate in a leadership context. We will discuss how to apply authentic leadership more practically in a bit, but for now, let's think about how this study-backed approach works in real-world applications.

Applying Authentic Leadership

Scenario: You're the leader of a marketing team that just launched a new product campaign. The initial feedback shows the campaign is not doing well, and the team is stressed. You need to address this using each component of authentic leadership:

---

3   Walumbwa, F. O., Avolio, B. J., Gardner, W. L., Wernsing, T. S., & Peterson, S. J. (2007). Authentic leadership: Development and validation of a theory-based measure. *Journal of Management, 34*(1), 89–126. https://doi.org/10.1177/0149206307308913

1. Self-awareness: Reflect on your own role in the campaign's performance. You realize that you pushed for a strategy that you were uncertain about, based on pressure from upper management.

2. Relational transparency: In your team meeting, you openly share your concerns about the strategy and admit your uncertainty.

3. Balanced processing: Before the meeting, you gather data from various sources—sales reports, customer feedback, and team input—to get a comprehensive view of the situation.

4. Internalized moral perspective: You decide to prioritize honesty and team growth over short-term results or appeasing upper management.

Based on this, you may share with the team that you take responsibility for the strategy. You would openly admit that you pushed for a strategy you didn't believe in and then commit to being more transparent about concerns in the future.

At the core, authenticity in leadership is being real—with yourself and with others. It involves being committed to knowing oneself and a willingness to share that true self, including all our imperfections and uncertainties. Authentic leaders understand their strengths, weaknesses, and impact. They lead as themselves rather than an idealized version of a leader.

THE POWER OF AUTHENTICITY

Countless studies have explored the impact of an authentic leader, and the results have shown a range of positive impacts for both individuals and organizations. The body of research on authentic leadership has grown exponentially since the early 2000s and has covered diverse cultures, industries, and organizational structures. Below are a few of the main findings:

1. Increased job commitment: Employees are more likely to stay with an organization when they perceive their leaders as authentic.[4]

2. Enhanced job satisfaction: Employees working with authentic leaders have greater satisfaction and fulfillment.[5]

3. Improved well-being: Employees working under authentic leaders report lower levels of stress, improved well-being, and less burnout.[6,7]

4. Heightened trust in leaders: Authentic leaders foster higher levels of trust toward leaders from team members.[8]

---

4   Milić, B., Grubić-Nešić, L., Kuzmanović, B., & Delić, M. (2017). The influence of authentic leadership on the learning organization at the organizational level: The mediating role of employees' affective commitment. *Journal of East European Management Studies, 22*(1), 9–38. https://doi.org/10.5771/0949-6181-2017-1-9

5   Monzani, L., Ripoll, P., & Peiró, J. M. (2014). The moderator role of followers' personality traits in the relations between leadership styles, two types of task performance and work result satisfaction. *European Journal of Work and Organizational Psychology, 24*(3), 444–461. https://doi.org/10.1080/1359432x.2014.911173

6   Rahimnia, F., & Sharifirad, M. S. (2014). Authentic leadership and employee well-being: The mediating role of attachment insecurity. *Journal of Business Ethics, 132*, 363–377. https://doi.org/10.1007/s10551-014-2318-1

7   Laschinger, H. K. S., & Fida, R. (2013). A time-lagged analysis of the effect of authentic leadership on workplace bullying, burnout, and occupational turnover intentions. *European Journal of Work and Organizational Psychology, 23*(5), 739–753. https://doi.org/10.1080/1359432x.2013.804646

8   Qiu, S., Alizadeh, A., Dooley, L. M., & Zhang, R. (2019). The effects of authentic leadership on trust in leaders, organizational citizenship behavior, and service quality in the Chinese hospitality industry. *Journal of Hospitality and Tourism Management, 40*, 77–87.

5. Enhanced individual performance: Employees demonstrate improved job performance working under authentic leaders.[9]

6. Effective organizational change: Authentic leaders are more effective in implementing change.[10]

The list goes on to include increased optimism, creativity, psychological safety, and resourcefulness.[11] These peer-reviewed studies underscore just how impactful authenticity as a leader is on one's teams, organizations, and individual employees.

By embracing and sharing their true self, leaders can cause a ripple effect that reaches all aspects of their organization—from the well-being of their individual employees to the bottom line. For relatable leaders, authenticity is a catalyst for building stronger connections, facilitating a positive work environment, and driving organizational success.

AUTHENTICITY ACROSS GENERATIONS AND GENDERS

With the abundance of research on the importance of authenticity in leadership, I was confident that "authentic" would be at the top

---

9 Duarte, A. P., Ribeiro, N., Semedo, A. S., & Gomes, D. R. (2021). Authentic leadership and improved individual performance: Affective commitment and individual creativity's sequential mediation. *Frontiers in Psychology, 12.* https://doi.org/10.3389/fpsyg.2021.675749

10 Avolio, B. J., Gardner, W. L., Walumbwa, F. O., Luthans, F., & May, D. R. (2004). Unlocking the mask: A look at the process by which authentic leaders impact follower attitudes and behaviors. *The Leadership Quarterly, 15*(6), 801–823. https://doi.org/10.1016/j.leaqua.2004.09.003

11 Polat, E., Arıcı, H. E., & Arasli, H. (2024). Authentic leadership: A systematic review and research agenda. *Ege Akademik Bakis (Ege Academic Review), 24*(3), 369–390. https://doi.org/10.21121/eab.240302

of the list in terms of what employees are seeking in a leader. It was...and wasn't. As a whole, authenticity was ranked lower than expected overall, coming in at number ten on a list of 18 leadership traits. However, there were significant differences when we broke down the data by gender and generation—especially gender. While women ranked "authentic" at number twelve, men considered it a top-three leadership quality.

There are likely several reasons why authenticity was not in the universal top three for all genders and generations. Perhaps those segments of the population believe we need to focus on other areas first, and that the more fundamental elements like respect and trust need to be established before authenticity can truly be appreciated in leadership roles. It may also be due to the challenges women face in being authentic at work, as research has shown that "women's authenticity is compromised by phenomena like the imposter phenomenon and impression management."[12] Women shine in leadership roles when they can be authentic, yet breaking through the barriers to do so is difficult.[13]

Despite these challenges, it's clear that authenticity is valued. According to a study, 62 percent of participants believe that leaders are following an outdated model wherein they don't share their human side, in spite of the fact that an overwhelming majority responded that a more relatable leader who shows their human side is more effective. Additionally, when asked to rate the importance of how leaders connect with them, "Employees want leaders who are authentic and transparent" was ranked the highest.

---

12 Howard, L. (2024). Authenticity and woman's leadership: A qualitative study of professional business services in the UK. *Journal of Work-Applied Management*. https://doi.org/10.1108/JWAM-09-2023-0092

13 Ibid.

The results indicate that authenticity's role in leadership is more layered than I initially thought—there go those assumptions again! Employees clearly believe authenticity is important and that it creates a more effective and connective leader. However, they may have higher priorities at the moment or believe that authenticity is not always possible for leadership. It should be noted that this doesn't diminish the value of authenticity; rather, it highlights that employees view it as part of a broader set of necessary leadership qualities, and recognize that it is more difficult for some to express than others.

PRACTICALLY AUTHENTIC—HOW TO LEAD

While the research clearly demonstrates the value of being authentic as a leader, it can be challenging to implement. How can leaders integrate authenticity into their daily interactions and communications? How can we combine transparency and humanity while remaining confident and assertive?

As we've discussed, scholars define authentic leadership as being self-aware, relationally transparent, balanced in decision-making, and guided by an internalized moral perspective. Translating academic concepts into practical, everyday leadership methods requires a bit more nuance. With that in mind, the following are four practical steps leaders can integrate to cultivate authentic leadership.

1. Develop Self-Awareness

Self-awareness is the foundation of leading authentically. If we aren't willing to be real with ourselves, we will never be capable of being real with others. A self-aware leader understands their strengths and weaknesses and understands how their words and actions impact others. One can become more self-aware by:

1. *Reflecting and observing*: Take time to be introspective regarding your thoughts, feelings, and reactions. Notice patterns in behaviors and emotions. You might recognize that you tend to become impatient during long meetings, or you notice that your mood impacts decision-making. You may also notice positive patterns, like how excited you get over a new idea or how you remain calm under pressure. By becoming aware of these tendencies, both positive and negative, you understand more about who you are and how real you are being.

2. *Seeking feedback*: Ask others for feedback and constructive criticism about how you show up in the world and how you lead. We can only self-assess to an extent, but to get a complete view of how we are perceived, it's important to seek input from others. For instance, you could utilize a 360-degree review from your team, peers, and management or have one-on-one sessions with those on your team you feel could provide valuable input.

3. *Being open to personal growth*: Acknowledge that there's always room for improvement and actively seek opportunities to learn and evolve. This could involve setting personal development goals, such as improving your emotional intelligence. You could enroll in leadership workshops, read books (ahem), or seek mentorships and masterminds from and with other leaders.

4. *Practicing mindfulness*: Engage in mindfulness techniques like meditation or journaling to increase present-moment awareness and emotional intelligence. For example, start

each day with a ten-minute meditation session to center yourself. There is an abundance of apps that offer guided meditations and mindfulness exercises.

These tactics will help you become more self-aware, where you will not only understand more about yourself but also your impact on others. Note that developing self-awareness is a continuous process—self-awareness begets more self-awareness. As you become more mindful, you'll find it easier to lead authentically, make decisions aligned with your values, and connect more genuinely with your team.

2. Show Vulnerability

Vulnerability in leadership isn't about oversharing or creating connections with no regard for boundaries; it's about sharing your human side. Being vulnerable has been defined in research as the state of being susceptible to harm or damage and is the willingness to be open and expose oneself to potential risks or harm in a trusting relationship.[14] Woah. That doesn't sound like a great move for a leader, does it? Exposing oneself to harm?

In the context of leadership, vulnerability manifests as the courage to be authentic—imperfections and all. It involves acknowledging uncertainties and being open about challenges. There are ways to start small in showing vulnerability:

- Share a personal story in your next meeting that demonstrates a point.
- Be honest about uncertainties or challenges around a project.

14 Nienaber, A., Hofeditz, M., & Romeike, P. D. (2015). Vulnerability and trust in leader-follower relationships. *Personnel Review*, *44*(4), 567–591. https://doi.org/10.1108/pr-09-2013-0162

- Express empathy when team members face difficulties.
- Acknowledge when you don't have all the answers and invite input from others.

The good news is that most employees believe their leaders are doing well in terms of vulnerability and humility generally (except for men, who feel their leaders could use some work in this area).

3. Encourage Open Communication

Open communication is essential to creating an environment where authenticity can thrive. As an authentic leader, fostering a culture where team members feel comfortable expressing their ideas and concerns is fundamental. This can be achieved by:

- Actively listening to your team
- Valuing diversity in ideas and team members
- Recognizing that open communication can occur through various channels.

There will be team members who will never speak up in a team meeting but will share freely in one-on-ones. There are times when a system or survey for anonymous feedback makes the most sense. Creating an atmosphere of open communication requires knowing your team and what would allow them to feel the safest to share in the most efficient way. Remember, it's not just about creating opportunities for dialogue—it's about showing that you're open to and appreciative of honest feedback and diverse viewpoints. By allowing your team to be authentic and real with you, you're reinforcing your own authenticity as a leader.

4. Stay True to Your Values

Authentic leadership is rooted in a strong sense of personal values and one's moral compass. Staying true to your values means that your actions align with your beliefs—even when it's hard, or there are outside pressures. You have a clear understanding of who you are and what you stand for, and your leadership reflects this.

Many leaders may already have a strong sense of their core values. If you're one of them, awesome—you're already a step ahead. However, it's always helpful to take a look at our values as they evolve over time. For those who are still defining their values or for leaders looking to revisit them, here are some strategies to help:

- *Reflect on your peaks and valleys.* Think about the times you felt most proud or most disappointed; what values were you honoring or compromising? For example, maybe you felt proud when you stood up for a colleague, which shows that fairness or loyalty could be a top value. Or, maybe you were disappointed when you had to rush a project and sacrifice quality, showing that excellence may be a core value. Taking a look at these moments can reveal what truly matters to you.

- *Consider your legacy.* This is possibly morbid but very effective: Ask yourself, what do you want to be remembered for? How would you want those who knew you to describe you? Would you want them to say, "She was kind and fair," or "They were innovative and pushed boundaries"? The qualities you hope to be remembered for can reflect your strongest values.

- *Use an assessment tool.* There are many online resources and exercises designed to help you identify your values.

Once you've identified your core values, compare your actions and decisions against them. It doesn't mean you're inflexible; it means you're consistent in aligning with what guides you.

By incorporating these four steps—developing self-awareness, showing vulnerability, encouraging open communication, and staying true to their values—leaders can cultivate authenticity in their interactions and communications.

BALANCING AUTHENTICITY AND PROFESSIONALISM

Raj had always prided himself on being an open book—as a friend, partner, and leader. He had developed strong relationships with the team at his startup and felt that honesty was imperative. However, he also learned that sometimes you can be a bit too honest.

It was the first Monday of the new month and new quarter, and he called a meeting of his top leaders to go over financials. After the team filed into the conference room, Raj took a deep breath and began:

"As you all know, I try to be as honest and transparent as possible with all of you. We are in a really tough spot right now. I just found out that we lost another major client over the weekend, and I'm worried about making payroll next month. I haven't slept in days." He went on, "My advisors and I have been arguing about the next steps and if we will even remain viable. I'm beginning to wonder if it's me, and I'm a fool for thinking I can run a startup." As Raj spoke, the team exchanged shocked and worried glances. The energy of the room became more and more tense. By the time Raj finished, the team looked shell-shocked.

In the days that followed, productivity plummeted. Rumors circulated, and employees began job hunting. Raj's intentions were good—he wanted to be authentic and transparent with his team. Yet, he failed to balance honesty with boundaries that protected him from unnecessary negative consequences.

Effective authentic leadership requires judgment and awareness. Asking the following questions can help find the right mix:

- Is this information necessary for my team to know? While honesty and transparency are important, do they need to know these details?

- How will this information likely affect my team? What is the impact? Will it increase stress and reduce productivity?

- Am I sharing this to benefit me or them? Make sure your sharing is rooted in leadership and not catharsis.

- Is this appropriate professionally? Your team does not receive the same information as your close friends.

- Is this the right time and place? Consider the setting and timing.

Further, even if the information passes all the above, in times of challenge (like with Raj), we need to determine how to frame the information constructively with the next steps. There will be times when the information you need to be transparent about is not positive. However, even difficult messages can be shared authentically while maintaining team morale. Here are some strategies:

1. Provide context. Discuss the broader picture, not just the result.

2. Be solution-oriented. Share the next steps.

3. Emphasize strengths. Focus on the positive aspects of the team and past achievements.

4. Set clear expectations. Outline what's needed from the team.

5. Show confidence. Show that you believe there will be a successful outcome.

Raj's experience was expensive—financially and energetically. He would spend years undoing the damage he did to the confidence in his leadership and the company. Moving forward, he worked on finding a middle ground—being genuine and transparent but also maintaining the professionalism and confidence his team needed in a leader.

Authenticity in leadership doesn't mean sharing every thought or emotion. It means being true to your values, honest in your communications, and genuine in your interactions, all while remaining professional.

A NOTE ABOUT MISTAKES

Early in his role, Jim Whitehurst, former CEO of software company Red Hat, made a decision to release a product that wasn't entirely open source—he believed they didn't have time to rewrite the code. The decision ended up backfiring; his team and customers disliked the product, and Red Hat ended up rewriting the code. What would have initially set them back a few months cost the company a year, causing frustration and anger within the team.

Instead of deflection or avoidance, Whitehurst owned up to his mistake. He explained his thinking to both the board and the employees, admitting he was wrong, and outlined the plan to address the issue. His transparency resonated with Red Hat employees, and many shared that they appreciated his explanation of his decision-making process. Whitehurst found that by admitting his mistake, he increased their trust in him and improved engagement.

My research revealed an interesting disconnect between the perceptions of employees and leaders when it comes to vulnerability and admitting mistakes, especially when broken down generationally. A few key points:

1. Younger supervisors felt strongly that leaders should admit their mistakes, while older leaders did not agree.

2. Millennials especially believe that leaders should admit their mistakes.

3. Generally, employees believe that leaders need to work on admitting their mistakes, with Gen Z, millennials, boomers, and women leading the charge (notably, almost 31 percent of all respondents believed admitting mistakes needed work by leaders).

4. Younger employees thought leaders who demonstrated mistakes made them easier to connect with.

This data suggests that supervisors may be underestimating the power of vulnerability in relation to their imperfections. However, it's necessary to approach the admission of mistakes carefully. If you've made a mistake that warrants sharing, be direct and prompt. Acknowledge it and explain without making excuses—as Whitehurst did. Most importantly, share and demonstrate how you plan to fix or have fixed the situation.

Remember, while admitting mistakes can demonstrate humility, accountability, and a commitment to growth, it should be done judiciously and with confidence in the ultimate outcome. It's essential to consider the impact on your team and organization as you decide how to share.

Do this	Not that
Be true to your values	Try to be someone you're not
Acknowledge when things are tough	Fake positivity
Share appropriate personal stories that relate to work	Overshare personal information or problems
Admit when you don't have all the answers	Pretend to know everything
Express genuine emotion	Always remain stoic
Discuss your own career journey, including setbacks	Present only a polished version of your professional path
Take the time to understand your team's needs and emotions	Keep an emotional distance

FINAL THOUGHTS

Authentic leadership is a powerful tool in the relatable leader's toolbox. Authentic leaders are genuine, transparent, and true to who they are and their values. Authenticity's impact on employees and organizations is undeniable: building trust, improving performance and satisfaction, increasing creativity and innovation—all part of creating a work environment where teams can thrive.

We need to remember that getting to a place as a leader where you feel you can be truly authentic can be a journey. It requires confidence and self-awareness, knowing that if you have the courage to be vulnerable and real, your teams will thrive. The future indeed belongs to leaders who dare to be human—those who can connect, communicate, and inspire through their genuine selves. Embrace your humanity, learn from your mistakes, and lead with integrity. Your team and your organization will be better for it.

CONNECTION CATALYSTS

Reflect on a time when a leader's authenticity (or lack thereof) significantly impacted you. How did it affect your performance and engagement?

_____
_____
_____
_____

Identify one area where you could be more authentic in your leadership. What's holding you back, and what's one small step you could take this week to be more genuine?

_____
_____
_____
_____

Think about your core values. How well do your daily leadership actions align with these values?

_____
_____
_____
_____

CHAPTER 5

Bridging Intention and Interpretation: Communication as Leadership

"Leadership isn't a megaphone; it's a dialogue."

The COVID-19 pandemic in 2020 changed work forever. The unprecedented and immediate shift to remote work forced companies to rethink everything overnight. Organizations that had never developed or allowed a work-from-home policy found themselves with an entirely remote workforce. As the crisis slowly ended and things returned to a "new normal," organizations began to realize that many of their employees preferred the flexibility of a work-from-home or hybrid schedule. This shift was in direct conflict with the desire of executives and has led to a multitude of debates and research regarding how efficient remote teams truly are.[1]

In January 2024, Internet Brands, the parent company of WebMD, found itself at the center of this struggle. The company

---

1   Ding, Y., & Ma, M. (2023). Return-to-office mandates. *SSRN Electronic Journal.* https://doi.org/10.2139/ssrn.4675401

spent over a year trying (and failing) to bring its workers back to the office on a hybrid schedule. In response, the company created a video featuring CEO Bob Brisco and other executives urging teams to return to the office. There was dancing and music, with an interesting attempt at levity, especially when combined with an explicit and terse statement from Brisco regarding the return to office plans. "We're not asking or negotiating at this point. We're informing," he said.

The video went viral, and the millions of views resulted in responses that included consistent comments about how "bizarre" and "cringe-worthy" the messaging was. The video was pulled offline, but it had already become an example of what not to do. Understandably, the leadership of many organizations prefer employees to be in office—at least some of the time, but to present an ultimatum juxtaposed with humor was not the way to communicate with their employees. The video was educational though, as it highlighted the ongoing struggles companies face in navigating the complexities of post-pandemic work and the potential pitfalls of mishandling leadership communication.

My research on relatable leadership generated several unexpected insights. However, the desire and demand for a leader who communicates honestly and openly was *not* surprising. Effective, respectful communication is essential in every area of our lives—professionally and personally. Developing our communication skills gives us stronger and healthier relationships, less conflict, and improved self-esteem. In my role as a communication consultant, I've witnessed firsthand the transformative power of effective leadership communication. One CEO I worked with saw employee engagement scores jump by 20 percent after implementing the strategies we'll discuss in this chapter. On the other hand, poor communication in the workplace has been found to impact job satisfaction, productivity, and stress.[2]

As a leader? Clear, consistent communication is the lifeblood of successful teams. It's how we share our visions, motivate our teams, and overcome challenges. This chapter will focus on communication as leadership and how to create a two-way street where teams feel seen and heard, and leaders engage in genuine exchanges.

DATA-DRIVEN DIALOGUE: KEY INSIGHTS

The importance of communication in becoming a relatable leader is a main finding from my research. "Communicates clearly" and "active listener" are ranked as the third and fourth most valued traits of a relatable leader. The emphasis on communication is neither unexpected nor temporary—the need for good communication is fundamental and forever. Clear communication and a leader who listens to you is an expectation that transcends age and gender, though there are a few variations that were notable. Let's break down these findings across different demographics.

Generations:

- Gen Z and boomers, despite the age gap, had identical rankings and mirrored the overall survey results as both groups rank "Communicates Clearly" at third and "Active Listener" at fourth.
- Millennials prioritized clear communication (third) but interestingly placed less emphasis on active listening (eighth) as compared to transparency (fourth).

---

2   Hoory, L. (2023, March 8). The state of workplace communication in 2025. *Forbes.* https://www.forbes.com/advisor/business/digital-communication-workplace/

- Gen X, sandwiched between millennials and boomers, flips the script. They value active listening (third) over clear communication (sixth), indicating a desire for leaders who take the time to understand their perspectives.

Additional research has shown that "today's young workers—ages twenty-one to thirty-four—place more value on having respectful communication in the workplace over trendy work perks. When young workers experience a culture of *respectful* engagement, they are more likely to experience occupational resilience."[3] This callback to respect highlights how critical communication is—not just in day-to-day productivity but in developing resilient teams.

Shifting our focus to differences by gender, another interesting pattern emerged:

- Women also reflected the overall results, ranking "Communicates Clearly" at third and "Active Listener" at fourth.
- Men ranked clear communication (fourth) over active listening (sixth) and placed authenticity and openness in their top five.

Beyond the ranking of traits, my research delved deeper into specific aspects of communication as a leader. When asked to rank the importance of how a leader communicates, "Leaders should actively listen to and recognize employees" came second only to "Trust is built through honest, transparent communication." When participants were asked to identify the single most

---

3   LaGree, D., Houston, B., Duffy, M., & Shin, H. (2023). The effect of respect: Respectful communication at work drives resiliency, engagement, and job satisfaction among early career employees. *International Journal of Business Communication, 60*(3), 844–864. https://doi.org/10.1177/23294 884211016529

important quality in a good leader, the top response was, "A great communicator who is honest, transparent, and listens to me."

Taken as a whole, the results paint a clear picture—effective communication—both in how leaders express and engage—isn't just desired, it's expected. Throughout this chapter, we'll explore how leaders can cultivate these essential communication skills to both meet and exceed these expectations.

THE LEADER'S TOOLKIT: FUNDAMENTAL COMMUNICATION STRATEGIES

As we've learned, effective communication is an absolute necessity for leaders, but what does it look like in practice? This section will focus on how leaders can, as the title of this chapter alludes to, bridge the gap between intention and interpretation and learn to communicate in a way that is both clearly understood and well-received. Whether you're leading a team of five or five thousand, whether you're navigating a sea of remote workers or maintain a fully occupied office, these tools will help you communicate more clearly, listen more actively, and connect more deeply with your team. Let's dive in and start building your communication toolkit through clear messaging, active listening, and consistency.

Mastering the Art of Clear Messaging

As we've discussed, "communicates clearly" ranked as the third most valued trait in a relatable leader according to my research, and while it is a quality that all employees desire, it is also an active, ongoing practice that leaders must develop (and refine). Let's break down what clear messaging looks like in action and the WHO—HOW—WHY approach to messaging that resonates.

WHO

Effective communication starts with understanding who you're speaking to. This goes beyond recognizing basic demographics—it requires a deeper dive into your audience's background, cultural context, and communication preferences. Consider the knowledge level of your team members—are they experts in their field or new hires? Be conscious of cultural differences that impact how your message is received. Recognize that different generations may have varying preferences for how they consume information. It can seem daunting to try and understand each individual team member, and there will be times when you have to generalize when communicating to large teams or your organization as a whole, but any insights into WHO they are will help your words resonate more effectively.

Action step: Before any significant communication, take time to reflect on your audience. For large or diverse teams, it can be helpful to create audience avatars, allowing you to step into your team member's shoes and create a message that resonates best.

HOW

Once you know your audience, it's time to create your message and decide *how* it is best delivered. As leaders, you often deal with sensitive issues, challenging situations, and complicated topics that can be not only hard to articulate but they can be stressful to deliver. The goal is to communicate effectively even when the subject matter is challenging, or the circumstances are difficult. It's when clear messaging isn't just a good idea; it's critical.

In all communication, start by using simplified language and try to break down complex ideas into smaller, more digestible parts. With sensitive topics, being direct but empathetic is your best bet while providing context to the bigger picture. Storytelling can also be a powerful tool. An anecdote or story can make a difficult message more relatable and understandable.

Lastly, don't underestimate the power of visual aids in helping to explain complicated or sensitive information. Charts, graphs, and infographics can present data in a way that people can more easily understand.

While these tools can enhance your message delivery, we need to remember that consistency is the thread that ties everything together. Consistency across mediums is key. Whether you're communicating in person, via email, or through other digital methods, it's important to make sure that your message lands the same.

Action step: In your next communication about a complex issue, share a draft with one to three members of your team to assess for clarity and impact.

WHY

Before any communication, take a moment to understand your purpose and reason for sharing. Ask yourself:

- What is the reason for this communication? Why am I sharing it?
- What do I want my team to know, feel, or do after receiving this message?
- How does this information align with our goals and purpose?

Reflection makes sure that your communication is necessary, purposeful, and valuable. We live in a world where we are all constantly bombarded by messages from all angles, so it helps to focus on what actually matters. Creating communication with purpose is paramount.

Maybe you're sharing an update on a project, and your "why" could be to help encourage and show recognition to the team. If you're implementing a new policy, your "why" could be to improve safety or efficiency. Your purpose guides the content, intention, and impact. Clear communication isn't just about what you say or how you say it—it's also about why you're saying it.

Action step: Before your next significant communication, take five minutes to write down your answers to these questions:

- What is the primary purpose of this message?
- What specific outcome am I hoping to achieve?
- How does this align with our broader goals?

Use these answers to guide the content and tone of your message.

Lastly, we need to remember that clear communication involves perpetual tweaking and adjusting. Create opportunities for regular feedback, allow for clarifying questions, and, most of all, be open to change.

A Deeper Dive into Active listening

Eighty percent of corporate communication resources are spent on speaking, yet listening is arguably the most critical skill for effective leadership.[4] The impact of listening is undeniable, yet the data shows that leaders are failing to truly hear their teams. A staggering 63 percent of employees feel their voice has been

---

4   Macnamara, J. (2016). The work and "architecture of listening": Addressing gaps in organization-public communication. *International Journal of Strategic Communication, 10*(2), 133–148. https://doi.org/10.1080/1553118x.2016.1147043

ignored by leadership.[5] This disconnect highlights an enormous gap in leadership practices *and* an opportunity for improvement. What happens when leaders listen? It's transformative.

There is no deeper human desire than to feel seen and heard.

When employees feel heard, they are more engaged, effective, and innovative, and they are 4.6 times more likely to feel empowered to perform to the best of their ability.[6,7] One of the ways employees experience meaningfulness in their work is when they are given confidence and the opportunity to be heard.[8] Combining these findings with my research that underscores the importance of active listening across all generations and genders, it becomes clear that active listening is at the core of a connected and collaborative culture.

As we discussed in Chapter 2, active listening is a key component of showing respect to your team members. The EARS approach was introduced:

E—Engage fully with your complete attention focused.

A—Ask questions to show curiosity and improve understanding.

R—Reflect back main points by paraphrasing or summarizing.

S—Suspend judgment and avoid interrupting.

---

5   *The Heard and the Heard-Nots.* (n.d.). https://workforceinstitute.ck.page/heardandheardnots

6   Ibid.

7   Ibid.

8   Newman, A., Donohue, R., & Eva, N. (2017). Psychological safety: A systematic review of the literature. *Human Resource Management Review, 27*(3), 521–535. https://doi.org/10.1016/j.hrmr.2017.01.001

This framework provides a solid foundation for active listening, but there's much more to explore about this essential aspect of leadership.

Active listening as a concept was initially developed by psychologist Carl Rogers in 1951 with the intention to create a person-centered therapy through a practice of being nonjudgmental, empathetic, and creative.[9] Rogers believed that, at its core, active listening was about developing a genuine connection with the client that was rooted in care. His intention was to make his clients feel truly heard and valued. The original construct was adapted (and arguably weakened) through its application in corporate communications. Rogers warned that many of the techniques we utilize in active listening, like paraphrasing, would be ineffective without the right mindset.[10] His belief was that true listening only occurred when the listener had the right attitude and cared about the person in front of them.

Based on the research, it can be argued that returning to the spirit of Rogers' definition may be the path we need to reconnect with our teams and create an environment where people feel truly heard. Rogers believed that effective listening required:

- Genuineness/authenticity
- Unconditional positive regard for the speaker
- Empathetic understanding[11]

For Rogers, the goal wasn't just to hear words but to create a safe psychological space where the person he was speaking

---

9   Rogers, C. R. (1951). *Client-Centered Therapy: Its Current Practice, Implications and Theory.* Boston, MA: Houghton Mifflin.

10   Ibid.

11   Rogers, C. R. (1961). *On Becoming a Person.* Boston, MA: Houghton Mifflin.

with felt truly heard. These core principles align with the EARS approach but go beyond just techniques.

In a corporate context, leaders can cultivate this level of listening, but it requires a shift in intention and a large dose of self-awareness. Here's how the EARS framework would be up-leveled by incorporating Rogers' principles:

- E—Engage fully: Beyond just focusing attention, this involves being genuinely present and authentic in the interaction. It means avoiding distractions (I often say we don't have phones. We have tiny computers that follow us everywhere) and bringing your whole self to the conversation.

- A—Ask questions: Asking questions aligns with Rogers' emphasis on empathetic understanding. Questions should come from a place of genuine curiosity to understand the speaker's perspective, not to lead or judge.

- R—Reflect back: While reflection is valuable, Rogers would emphasize that the reflection should demonstrate a deep, empathetic understanding of not just the words but the intention and meaning behind them.

- S—Suspend judgment: This closely aligns with Rogers' concept of unconditional positive regard. It involves accepting the speaker's perspective without evaluation, creating a safe space for open expression.

If we were able to uplevel the EARS approach with Rogers' deeper principles, leaders could move beyond surface-level listening techniques and create truly transformative connections with their teams. This approach can yield powerful results, as illustrated by the story of David Abney at UPS.

In 1974, nineteen-year-old David Abney began his career at UPS, loading packages onto vans at night to earn extra money while studying. Over the next four decades, he climbed the corporate ladder, eventually becoming CEO. Abney attributes much of his success to intentionally listening to employees.

When he was named CEO, one of Abney's first initiatives was to embark on a worldwide listening tour. He gave employees and customers alike the opportunity to voice their opinions on the company and its direction. It wasn't just a symbolic gesture. As one anonymous UPS employee shared, "When David issued a call for ideas, many of which were actually implemented, it was almost earth-shattering. We couldn't believe leadership was finally listening and taking action on our recommendations."

Abney's approach embodies the principles of active listening we've discussed. By genuinely seeking to understand employees' perspectives and acting on their input, he created a transformative connection between leadership and employees, increasing engagement and trust from employees who felt truly heard and valued.

While challenging, this standard of listening has incredible potential. Leaders who can embody Rogers' principles of genuineness, unconditional positive regard, and empathetic understanding have the potential to not only improve individual relationships but to reshape organizational cultures.

It's important to note that active listening is not just a communication technique but a powerful way to demonstrate respect. When leaders truly listen, they show that they value their team members' perspectives and contributions. This respect, in turn, nurtures trust and encourages more open communication.

Consistency in Leadership Communication

As we explored in Chapter 3, consistency is one of the key pillars of trustworthy leadership and involves an alignment of one's words and actions. When it comes to communication, consistency takes on additional elements. Let's build on those previous concepts and discover how consistency specifically applies to leadership communication.

Consistency in communication includes:

- Maintaining messaging across platforms and mediums: Whether you are communicating face-to-face or digitally, the message is the same.
- Regular communication: Teams need to be able to rely on a predictable pattern of information—whether that is in person or digital, though in-person conversations are particularly effective. Gallup found that a leader having one meaningful conversation per week with each team member creates high-performance relationships more than any other activity.[12]
- Consistent tone and style: While adapting to different audiences is necessary, maintaining a consistent overall communication style helps to maintain an authentic leadership voice.
- Following through on commitments: When leaders promise to communicate something by a certain time or in a certain way, they absolutely have to deliver on that promise.

---

12 Harter, J. (2024, June 23). In new workplace, US employee engagement stagnates. *Gallup*.https://www.gallup.com/workplace/608675/new-workplace-employee-engagement-stagnates.aspx

When leaders communicate consistently, they create a sense of stability and reliability. It reduces uncertainty and unnecessary anxiety. Consistent communication also shows respect for the team by keeping them informed and in the loop. This level of communication requires effort and planning. Here are some practical ways to develop consistent communication practices in your leadership role:

- Schedule regular check-ins. Set up recurring team meetings and one-on-ones to ensure consistent touchpoints. Whether they are weekly, monthly, or quarterly, regular meetings create a rhythm teams can rely on.
- Establish communication channels. Determine the best platforms for different types of information (for example, use email for updates, team meetings for discussions, and intranet for company news).
- Use templates. For common messages, consider creating templates to maintain consistency in tone and format.
- Seek feedback. Regularly ask your team about the effectiveness of your communication and be willing to adjust as needed.

Remember, consistency doesn't equal rigidity. You can (and should) still be flexible and adapt to different situations and feedback while maintaining a consistent core message and communication style. By walking the talk and demonstrating consistency in your leadership communication, you'll build stronger connections with your team.

MANAGING EXPECTATIONS THROUGH COMMUNICATION

It's impossible to write a book on leadership and not address expectations. Successful leadership involves clearly defining and expressing expectations to guide team performance. Yet, despite its importance, creating clear expectations is something many organizations struggle with. Gallup has tracked employee expectations for decades, and *currently, less than half of employees know what is expected of them at work.* That's down from 56 percent immediately before the pandemic and 61 percent in 2015.[13] This downward trend indicates that there is a growing need to focus on how leaders and their teams communicate when it comes to what is expected in their roles.

Effective leaders understand the importance of clearly communicating expectations and goals. They establish specific, measurable objectives, prioritize check-ins to address questions and offer feedback, and consistently reinforce expectations across all levels of the organization.

It should also be noted that expectations can be a powerful tool—for both the employee and the organization. The Pygmalion effect is a psychological phenomenon first researched in the classroom, where it was discovered that high expectations can lead to improved performance.[14] Further studies have shown that when leaders communicate their expectations and confidence in a team's capabilities, a self-fulfilling prophecy of success can result. The

13 Gallup, Inc. (2024b, October 2). Global indicator: Employee engagement. *Gallup.*https://www.gallup.com/394373/indicator-employee-engagement.aspx

14 Rosenthal, R., & Jacobson, L. (1968). *Pygmalion in the Classroom: Teacher Expectation and Pupils' Intellectual Development.* New York: Holt, Rinehart and Winston, Inc.

more defined, focused, and ambitious a goal is, the better the performance tends to be.[15] However, we need to balance this with the other aspects of expectation management—clear goal-setting, regular feedback, and transparent communication about challenges. When combined, these practices create an environment for positive results.

Ultimately, effective expectation management is about creating an environment where every team member understands their role and goals. As we move forward in an ever-changing work landscape, the ability to clearly communicate and manage expectations will remain a crucial skill for relatable and effective leaders.

THE COMMUNICATION CHAMELEON: ADAPTING TO YOUR AUDIENCE

"Alright, team, let's hear those brilliant ideas!" Keisha opened the meeting. "Don't be shy; there are no bad contributions here!" As the executive director of an educational non-profit for the past seven years, Keisha has built a close-knit team through her passionate leadership and open communication. She believed that she knew her team well and that they felt comfortable sharing ideas during the weekly brainstorming sessions.

A major new project arose to secure a new funding source, and Keisha noticed that the meetings were not leading to the type of innovative ideas she had grown to expect from her team. In frustration, she decided to try a different approach and scheduled

---

15   Locke, E. A., & Latham, G. P. (2013). Goal setting theory, 1990. In E. A. Locke & G. P. Latham (Eds.), *New Developments in Goal Setting and Task Performance* (pp. 3–15). New York, NY: Routledge.

one-on-one meetings with her most creative team members. The results were shocking (and lucrative).

Mark, a community outreach coordinator, began, "I've been thinking, what if we created an interactive dashboard that visually shows the connection between our programs and community improvement?"

"Mark, that's fantastic!" Keisha exclaimed. "Why haven't you mentioned this in our team meetings?" Mark shifted uncomfortably. "I...I always feel like I can't jump in fast enough. By the time I'm able to get my thoughts together, the conversation moves on."

Maya, a self-proclaimed introvert and program evaluator, shared in her session with Keisha, "Have you ever thought about partnering with local artists to create murals and street art that showcase our impact? It could be a powerful visual representation of our work in the community and an element we could add to our application."

Keisha replied, "Wow. Maya, I love that! I'm so happy we were able to chat today," Maya smiled shyly, "I have a lot of ideas, but I have to admit that in big groups, it's hard for me to speak up."

The conversations were not only pivotal in creating a successful grant application but also eye-opening for Keisha. She realized that while innovation and creativity could result from large meetings, there are times when she may have been silencing some of her most valuable team members.

Keisha immediately transformed how their meetings were conducted—from sending out agendas in advance so the team could prepare their thoughts to offering one-on-one sessions for anyone who may not feel comfortable speaking up. The results were transformational. Engagement rose, productivity soared, and Keisha's relationship with her team became stronger than ever.

One of the most vital elements of leadership communication is recognizing that it is often less about the words you say and more about the environment surrounding them. Understanding and respecting the nuances of personalities involved is essential—from the introverts who may need more one-on-one conversations to the extroverts who thrive in crowded conference rooms.

Equally important is adapting the type of communication methods, both for in-person and remote teams.

Screen Time vs. Face Time: Optimizing Your Communication Medium

We live in a digital age, yet we maintain a diverse pool of generations in our workforce with differing views on what type of communication is most effective. While some team members prefer in-person conversations, others are more comfortable using digital channels like Slack or email. My research in this area was not surprising. When prompted with the statement, "I'd rather have a virtual conversation over face to face," millennials and Gen Z leaders and employees alike agreed, while boomers and Gen X strongly disagreed.

With 58 percent of the teams working remotely, 55 percent in hybrid settings and only 20 percent entirely on-site, it's a challenge for leaders to develop a strategy for communications that maintains a cohesive team while reaching people in the way they prefer and in a way that results in the most productivity.[16] In many cases, the shift to remote and hybrid work has required a larger percentage of digital communications. Without video calls, emails, and texts, team members wouldn't feel informed, heard, and connected.

---

16   Hoory, 2023.

However, this shift comes at a price. We have to recognize that zooming out is real—six out of every ten employees feel that communicating digitally is a key factor in burnout. The expectation that employees need to be constantly connected blurs the boundaries between home and work, creating an imbalance, with 58 percent of workers reporting that digital communication makes them feel the need to be more available.[17]

This new reality demands flexibility and adaptability above all. Leaders need to assess the needs and preferences of their teams to determine how to best leverage communication methods. Here are some strategies for effective digital communication regardless of where your team operates from:

- Create clear guidelines. Set expectations (and permissions) for response times to ensure everyone is on the same page and avoids miscommunication.
- Develop a mix of methods. Combine real-time meetings, one-on-ones, and asynchronous tools like Slack to allow for different work styles and preferences.
- Provide training. Offer communication skills training to help team members improve their interpersonal skills, especially for those with social anxiety. This can include workshops, seminars, or coaching sessions.
- Regularly assess and adjust. Continually gather feedback from team members about communication strategies and be willing to adjust.
- Incorporate in-person elements. When possible, include in-person meetings or gatherings to strengthen team bonds and improve communication. Even yearly face-to-face meetings or retreats significantly boost team cohesion.

17   Ibid.

Digital tools have revolutionized workplace communication, but they are not one-size-fits-all. We have to work to create a communication strategy that connects in a way that respects and resonates in order to build a team that is actually connected, not just electronically.

Inclusive Communication: Engaging Neurodivergent Team Members

An estimated 15 percent to 20 percent of the population is estimated to be neurodivergent, defined as someone whose brain and cognitive development is different from the typical range, including but not limited to attention-deficit disorders, autism spectrum disorder, and dyslexia.[18],[19] These differences can significantly impact how individuals process information, communicate, and interact in the workplace.

Recognizing neurodiversity is foundational for creating an inclusive work environment. Neurodivergent individuals often bring unique strengths to their roles, such as creative thinking, enhanced memory capability, and passion.[20] However, they may also face challenges in relation to workplace communications.

Common communication challenges for neurodivergent team members can include:

- Difficulty interpreting non-verbal cues or social nuances

---

18 Doyle, N. (2020). Neurodiversity at work: A biopsychosocial model and the impact on working adults. *British Medical Bulletin, 135*(1), 108–125. https://doi.org/10.1093/bmb/ldaa021

19 Shah, P. J., Boilson, M., Rutherford, M., Prior, S., Johnston, L., Maciver, D., & Forsyth, K. (2022). Neurodevelopmental disorders and neurodiversity: Definition of terms from Scotland's National Autism Implementation Team. *The British Journal of Psychiatry, 221*(3), 577–579. https://doi.org/10.1192/bjp.2022.43

20 Doyle, 2020.

- Sensory sensitivities in bright, busy, or loud environments
- Challenges with unstructured or ambiguous instructions
- Preference for literal language over figurative speech
- Difficulty with on-the-spot conversations and/or public speaking

To bridge these gaps and effectively communicate, relatable leaders should offer the following:

1. Clear messaging: Use clear and specific language. Avoid ambiguity and figures of speech. Provide step-by-step instructions for tasks.

2. Flexible delivery: Offer the communication channel that best resonates. Some neurodivergent individuals may prefer written communication over verbal or vice versa.

3. Structured meeting environments: Use agendas, provide materials in advance, and (try to) stick to scheduled time frames. This helps all team members, but especially those who struggle with unpredictability.

4. Sensory sensitive environments: When possible, consider lighting, temperature, sounds, and other environmental factors that might affect comfort and concentration.

Equally, it is essential that the overall environment is respectful and considerate. Encourage team members to be aware of neurodiversity and foster a culture of acceptance and support. By demonstrating flexibility and understanding, relatable leaders can build stronger connections with their neurodivergent team members and create a more inclusive, innovative, and effective work environment for all.

Try This: Adapting Communication Styles

Scenario: You need to announce a major change in project direction to your team. You have:

- Alex: A detail-oriented analyst who prefers data-driven decisions
- Bea: A big-picture thinker who likes to understand the "why"
- Carlos: A people-focused team player concerned about group dynamics

How would you adapt your communication for each team member?

- Alex: Prepare a detailed report with data supporting the change. Schedule a one-on-one to walk through the numbers.
- Bea: Start with the long-term vision. Explain how this change aligns with company goals and market trends.
- Carlos: Emphasize how the team will navigate this change together. Discuss the support systems in place and how roles might evolve.

The core message remains the same, but the delivery is tailored to each individual's preferences and needs.

FINAL THOUGHTS

Effective communication goes beyond sharing information; it's about creating understanding, fostering trust, and inspiring action. The research clearly shows that across all generations and genders, employees value leaders who can communicate clearly and listen actively. Remember that great communication is an ongoing practice that requires continuous evolution. Be open to feedback, willing to adjust your approach, and strive to create an environment where every team member feels heard and valued. By focusing on your communication skills, you'll not only become a more relatable leader but also build a more engaged, productive, and innovative team.

CONNECTION CATALYSTS

What's one listening technique you will implement in the next team meeting to ensure all voices feel actively heard?

_____

_____

_____

_____

What's one way you can make your next team meeting more inclusive for both introverts and extroverts?

_____

_____

_____

_____

Reflect on a recent miscommunication with your team. What could you have done differently to bridge the gap between your intention and their interpretation?

_____

_____

_____

_____

PART THREE

INSPIRE

CHAPTER 6

Recognition: Elevating Engagement Through Appreciation

*"Leadership isn't just about setting goals; it's
about witnessing every step on the journey and
acknowledging wins that fuel the climb."*

"Congratulations, Maria," a sharply dressed young executive shared. "We wanted to thank you for your years of dedication." Maria beamed; at sixty-eight, she had dedicated nearly four decades of service to the insurance agency she had helped build from a small two-person office into a large successful regional firm with a sprawling campus. Maria hadn't planned on staying as long as she did, and she never intended to spend her career in insurance, but she had become dedicated to the clients and colleagues who had grown into family over the years.

The years hadn't always been easy; Maria survived economic downturns, massive shifts in technology, and several personal struggles. As she stood there in a room filled with her colleagues, Maria's mind raced with memories of late nights pouring over new regulations, networking events in the community, and the relationships she had built over the years.

As the applause died down, a small, beautifully wrapped package was presented to her. Maria's heart rate quickened as she carefully unwrapped the gift—secretly hoping for a Tiffany blue box beneath the paper.

"We hope this shows our appreciation for your years of service," the executive shared.

Maria's heart sank as she revealed a small scented candle engraved with "In Gratitude for Your Exceptional Service." She struggled to stay composed and hoped her face didn't betray her, barely able to speak. She whispered, "Oh...how nice," while holding back tears.

The executive failed to notice her disappointment, "We thought it was fitting—you sure know how to brighten up your workspace. We just can't light it here, obviously," he said with a chuckle. "Thank you, Maria. Now, let's all get back to work, shall we?"

As the crowd dispersed, Tom, Maria's closest friend in the office, approached Maria, shaking his head. "A candle? Really? I'm so sorry, Maria. That's insane. You deserve so much more. This just shows how out of touch they've become."

Maria returned to her desk, putting the small offensive candle next to her monitor. She was heartbroken. She couldn't help but feel the shift in energy around her work. A place she had called home for forty years now felt foreign and cold.

Maria went on to work two more years at the company, but her commitment and passion were gone. It wasn't obvious or disruptive—Maria was far too professional for that—but all the extra efforts she had made, from mentoring younger employees to overtime without question (or compensation) to going above and beyond to find creative solutions to problems were gone. She did her work and went home. What was once a calling now felt like just a job. The company continued to do well, but it had lost something invaluable—an employee's heartfelt commitment.

Maria's story is a reminder of how impactful recognition is to our teams and how poorly executed recognition can destroy motivation and engagement—even in the best employees. It begs the question: How can we effectively motivate and recognize employees across different generations to make sure they remain encouraged and engaged? Throughout this chapter, we'll explore how each generation feels about recognition, including actionable insights for leaders to create meaningful recognition that actually lands.

UNDERSTANDING RECOGNITION: A MULTIFACETED APPROACH

Before we dive into the research and practical applications of recognition in the workplace, it's necessary to understand that recognition itself is not a one-dimensional concept. Brun and Dugas (2008) identify four distinct forms of recognition practices:

1. Personal recognition: Appreciating employees' individual qualities and the passion they bring to their roles. Speaks to an employee's value as a person, not just a worker.

2. Recognition of work practices: Focusing on how employees are performing at their jobs, including capabilities and professional background. This type of recognition acknowledges creativity, innovation, and improvement at work.

3. Recognition of job dedication: Recognizing the effort shown by an employee or team, even when the results don't meet expectations. This form of recognition values the process as just as much as the outcome.

4. Recognition of results: Recognition of the end product of employees' work and their contribution to success. This is oftentimes the most visible form of recognition, but it shouldn't be the only one.[1]

Understanding these different recognition practices can inspire leaders to form a more comprehensive view of when recognition is appropriate and how it can be expressed. It encourages a more inclusive approach that goes beyond only celebrating wins, allowing leaders to:

- Recognize the whole person, not just their output
- Appreciate the process and effort, not just the end result
- Acknowledge skills and methods, not just achievement
- Create a culture of continuous appreciation, not just recognition for major successes

As we explore the research and generational differences in how recognition is perceived and received, we need to remember that effective recognition often involves a combination of these practices. By understanding and implementing various forms of recognition, leaders can create a more holistic strategy that reaches all employees—across all generations.

Research-based Recognition

Recognition isn't just about grand gestures or monetary rewards. It's about creating an environment where employees feel valued, respected, and inspired to give their best. It's also about recognizing that different individuals and generations may be driven

---

1   Brun, J., & Dugas, N. (2008). An analysis of employee recognition: Perspectives on human resources practices. *The International Journal of Human Resource Management, 19*(4), 716–730. https://doi.org/10.1080/095 85190801953723

by different factors. Research has consistently demonstrated the many benefits of employee recognition. Studies have shown that recognition can serve as a protective buffer against burnout and emotional exhaustion.[2] It's been identified as a key driver of motivation, identity formation, and meaningful work experiences.[3] Organizations that prioritize employee recognition have reported higher levels of employee engagement, improved performance, and lower turnover rates.[4] Recognized workers are 3.7 times as likely to be engaged.[5] Beyond driving engagement and performance, recognition also contributes to employees' psychological well-being, and conversely, when an employee is not recognized, it can cause stress.[6]

Moreover, recognition acts as a form of positive feedback, reinforcing desired behaviors. According to principles of operant conditioning, behaviors that are acknowledged and rewarded are more likely to be repeated.[7] This creates a positive feedback loop, encouraging valuable behaviors.

2 Renger, D., Miché, M., & Casini, A. (2020). Professional recognition at work: The protective role of esteem, respect, and care for burnout among employees. *Journal of Occupational and Environmental Medicine, 62*(3), 202–209. https://doi.org/10.1097/jom.0000000000001782

3 Brun & Dugas, 2008.

4 Towers Watson. (2012). *Global Workforce Study: Engagement at Risk: Driving Strong Performance in a Volatile Global Environment.* https://employeeengagement.com/wp-content/uploads/2012/11/2012-Towers-Watson-Global-Workforce-Study.pdf

5 Gallup & Workhuman. (2024). *The Human-Centered Workplace: Building Organizational Cultures that Thrive.* https://www.gallup.com/analytics/472658/workplace-recognition-research.aspx

6 Ryan, R. M., & Deci, E. L. (2000). Self-determination theory and the facilitation of intrinsic motivation, social development, and well-being. *American Psychologist, 55*(1), 68–78. https://doi.org/10.1037/0003-066X.55.1.68

7 Skinner, B. F. (1953). *Science and Human Behavior.* New York, NY: Macmillan.

Despite all we know about the power of recognition, it turns out only 34 percent of employees say their company actually has a recognition program.[8] Backing up this statistic, the research found that 81 percent of managers and leaders admit recognition is not a major strategic priority at their company.[9] This is more than just a missed opportunity—it's a large gap between what we know works and what's actually happening in most workplaces. It's like knowing exercise is good for you but never bothering to put on your running shoes. The good news? This means there's plenty of room for improvement, and relatable leaders can stand out by getting recognition right.

However, implementing effective recognition isn't as straight-forward as it might seem. While the benefits of recognition are well-established in research studies, my study uncovered some surprising nuances in how different generations and genders perceive and value recognition in the workplace. These findings challenge some common assumptions about the types of recognition employees are looking for and show that there is a need for relatable leaders to be more personalized in how we tackle recognition of our teams.

One of the most interesting discoveries was that recognition, while notable, didn't rank as highly as other leadership qualities overall, such as respect, trust, and clear communication across all demographics. However, when we dive deeper into the data, patterns emerged that revealed some fascinating insights on how different groups value recognition.

---

8   Gallup & Workhuman, 2024.

9   Workhuman. (2022, June 28). *6 Ways Recognition Drives Impact*. https://www.workhuman.com/resources/reports-guides/6-ways-recognition-drives-impact/

For starters, baby boomers placed a higher premium on recognition compared to their younger counterparts. They ranked recognition of accomplishments as one of their top five most important leadership qualities. For older employees, acknowledging their contributions and achievements is especially important to keep them engaged.

In comparison, Gen Z ranked recognition the lowest out of all age groups at number thirteen out of seventeen traits. This finding challenges the common narrative that younger employees are constantly seeking validation and praise. It also hints at the shift we are seeing in workplace values, where younger generations are being driven by purpose, personal growth, and work–life balance as opposed to praise.

My study yielded particularly revealing insights when respondents were asked to rank various aspects of leadership communication. The resulting hierarchy painted an eye-opening picture for the workforce as a whole:

1. Trust is built through honest, transparent communication.

2. Leaders should actively listen to and *recognize* employees.

3. Leaders should make employees feel valued as individuals.

4. Leaders should be open to feedback, development, and growth.

5. Leaders should make employees feel heard and understood.

6. Leaders should admit their mistakes.

7. Leaders should adapt their communication styles to connect with different employees.

8. *Personalized, meaningful recognition* is impactful for employees.

9. *Public recognition* from leaders is highly motivating for employees.

10. Employees disengage without positive reinforcement and *recognition.*

Recognition was purposefully seeded throughout the statements, yet three out of four were ranked the lowest. Additionally, the highest ranking was coupled with active listening and may be a false positive—we already know active listening is one of the highest-valued traits for all generations.

Does this mean recognition is insignificant? No, similarly to when we discussed the importance of respect over more "popular" leadership principles, recognition is *always* a necessary part of the equation, but not at the expense of the other leadership qualities that are more foundational. In fact, this finding underscores a crucial point—recognition should be viewed as part of a comprehensive approach to leadership rather than a standalone solution to engagement. Just as respect forms the foundation upon which other leadership qualities can thrive, recognition can amplify other indispensable qualities of a great leader. Moreover, the lower ranking of standalone recognition statements suggests employees are looking for more than just applause. They want a leader who is multifaceted and one who can ensure that the recognition they provide hits the mark.

PERSONALIZING RECOGNITION: ONE SIZE DOESN'T FIT ALL

While my study revealed that recognition may not be the top priority for younger employees, it still remains a primary element of leadership. The key lies in tailoring recognition to the individual rather than relying on a one-size-fits-all approach. At its core, personalized recognition is a manifestation of respect, which, as we know, is the foundation of everything. It shows that you not only notice an employee's contributions but also understand and value their individual preferences and motivations. By tailoring recognition to each team member, you demonstrate a deep respect for their uniqueness and reinforce how important they are to the organization.

Elena approached me after I wrapped up my keynote for emerging healthcare leaders. She began, "Rachel, I really connected with your talk—especially the part around recognition. I know I personally like to be recognized by leadership, but I think my efforts to recognize my team are failing." Elena elaborated that her company had a formal program featuring monthly awards celebrated via intranet announcements and gift cards, "but it doesn't seem to be working, especially with the younger members of my team. I tried turning our team meetings into a bit of a celebration, but that was even worse."

I nodded encouragingly as I had an idea of what was coming next. She continued, "There's Aiden, one of our Gen Z nurses. He's brilliant, but whenever he wins an award in our staff meetings, he looks like he would rather disappear through the floor. And there are others that just don't seem to care one way or the other."

"In terms of Aiden, have you ever chatted with him to see what type of recognition he'd prefer?" I replied. Elena's eyes widened. "I...I'm embarrassed to say I haven't. I just assumed everyone loves to win something."

"I get it," I replied. "But we've learned through research and experience that in order for recognition to work, it has to be personalized. If the awards aren't working, a few direct questions could find you something more motivating." We chatted for a bit longer, brainstorming ideas for how Elena could create a more personalized approach to recognition within her team. A few weeks later, I received the email below:

> Rachel,
>
> I wanted to update you on what happened after our chat. I took your advice and had one-on-one conversations with each team member about how they prefer to be recognized. It was MIND BLOWING! We've since implemented a "menu" where team members can choose how they'd like to be appreciated. The change in team morale has been incredible. Even our more reserved team members seem more engaged and motivated.
>
> Thank you!!
> Elena

Elena's experience highlights a fundamental point: Recognition isn't just about the act itself but about how it's received. As leaders, our job is to be curious, to ask questions, and to truly understand what makes our team members feel valued and appreciated. It's about creating a culture where recognition is not just frequent but meaningful.

Looking for new ways to offer recognition? Check out this recognition menu for inspiration:

Professional Growth	Work–Life Enhancement	Public Recognition	Personalized Appreciation	Experiential Rewards
Lead a new project or initiative	Extra paid time off	Spotlight in company newsletter	Private recognition in a one-on-one meeting	Tailored experience vouchers
Attend a relevant conference or workshop	Flexible scheduling for a month	Acknowledgment at all hands/ staff meetings	Personal thank-you note from supervisor or CEO	Concert or event tickets
One-on-one career planning session with a senior leader	Work-from-home days (for applicable roles)	Peer-nominated awards	Meaningful gift based on personal interests	Team-building outings
Subscription to online learning platform of choice	Personal wellness day	Digital achievement badges	Surprise favorite treats	Travel getaway vouchers
Mentorship pairings	Wellness program access	Social media highlights	Thank-you videos	Dining gift certificates

The only limitation is your creativity. And when in doubt? Ask them—"How would you like to be recognized for your great work?"

There are three steps to sincere recognition:

1. Be specific. Clearly identify and articulate the particular action, behavior, or achievement you're recognizing. Avoid vague or generic praise.

2. Explain the impact. Describe how the employee's contribution affected the team, the organization, or the broader mission. This helps the employee understand the significance of their work.

3. Express genuine appreciation. Convey your authentic gratitude for their effort and contribution. This can be done through your tone, body language, and choice of words.

As with everything in leadership, it all comes back to respect. Ninety-two percent of employees who believe their leader's recognition is insincere and inauthentic also believe that they are not treated with respect at work.[10] Conversely, workers who view their leader's recognition as authentic have a seven times increase in feeling respected on the job.[11]

Personalized and authentic recognition is a powerful tool for relatable leaders. However, it doesn't exist in isolation. When it's done poorly, it can undercut the foundation of trust and respect that great leaders work to build, as in Maria's case. When it's done well, it amplifies those other qualities and helps engage teams.

By understanding recognition as part of a larger leadership strategy, we can create environments where appreciation is woven into the fabric of daily work life, enhancing both individual and team performance.

FOSTERING A CULTURE OF MUTUAL APPRECIATION

While personalized recognition from leadership is necessary, it's only one piece of the appreciation puzzle. To create a truly engaging work environment, recognition should flow not just from the top down but also horizontally among peers. Some of the most meaningful recognition isn't from leaders but from our colleagues who witness and value our day-to-day efforts. Peer-to-peer recognition has a significant effect on teams, enhancing teamwork,

---

10   Maese, E., & Lloyd, C. (2023, July 18). Is your employee recognition really authentic? *Gallup*. https://www.gallup.com/workplace/508208/employee-recognition-really-authentic.aspx

11   Ibid.

collaboration, and overall organizational culture.[12] Research has shown that it can also improve performance and encourage openness and transparency.[13] Even more interesting are the unexpected benefits of peer-to-peer recognition, including:

- Reduced mistakes: The "Hawthorne effect" in action—people work harder and more carefully when they are supervised, even if that supervision is their own peers[14] and even when that supervision is related to acknowledging great work.
- Boosted performance through self-reflection: Nominating colleagues encourages employees to look at their own performance at work, leading to improved efficiency.
- Improved talent management: Peer review can be a valuable tool for remote performance appraisals and allows for the discovery of hidden talent within the organization.[15]

By implementing peer-to-peer recognition programs, organizations can create a more positive, supportive work environment where employees feel valued not just by leadership but by their colleagues as well. This mutual appreciation strengthens team

12 Rusin, N., & Szandała, T. (2024). The power of peer recognition points: Does it really boost employee engagement? *Strategic HR Review*. https://doi.org/10.1108/SHR-06-2024-0040

13 Anthony-McMann, P. E., Ellinger, A. D., Astakhova, M., & Halbesleben, J. R. B. (2016). Exploring different operationalizations of employee engagement and their relationships with workplace stress and burnout. *Human Resource Development Quarterly, 28*(2), 163–195. https://doi.org/10.1002/hrdq.21276

14 McCarney, R., Warner, J., Iliffe, S., Van Haselen, R., Griffin, M., & Fisher, P. (2007). The Hawthorne Effect: A randomised, controlled trial. *BMC Medical Research Methodology, 7*. https://doi.org/10.1186/1471-2288-7-30

15 CAEL. (2016, May 26). Pros and cons of peer review in workplace. *CAEL*. https://www.cael.org/resouces/pathways-blog/pros-and-cons-of-peer-review-in-the-workplace

bonds, increases job satisfaction, and ultimately contributes to a more engaged and productive workforce.

Let's explore how some leading companies have implemented successful peer-to-peer recognition initiatives:

Zappos—Employees can award an extra fifty dollars to a coworker each month for "WOWing" them. They also have a company currency called "Zollar" that can be spent on things like movie tickets or charitable donations.

Southwest Airlines—Employees use the SWAG (Southwest Airlines Gratitude) program to send each other "Kick Tails" notes of appreciation or nominate peers for awards with SWAG Points redeemable for travel rewards.

Typeform—Employees receive "typecoins" each month to show appreciation to teammates. These rewards can be converted to gift cards or cash.

American Airlines—The "Nonstop Thanks" platform, accessible via mobile app, allows team members to share appreciation and send eCards. Managers also use it to share positive customer feedback.

Cisco—The "Connected Recognition" program enables employees to nominate peers for various awards through an online platform. Rewards can accumulate significantly and be used for luxuries like upscale vacations.

These examples demonstrate a few of the innumerable ways organizations can create a successful peer-to-peer recognition program. They also show how technology can play a role in rolling out recognition programs that may otherwise seem overwhelming. Digital platforms make it easier to implement, track, and manage recognition initiatives, especially in large or geographically diverse organizations. They provide a streamlined system for employees to give and receive recognition easily.

When implementing a peer-to-peer recognition program, consider the following best practices:

1. Make it accessible. Ensure the recognition platform is user-friendly and easily accessible to all employees, whether through a mobile app, intranet, or integrated into existing communication tools.

2. Encourage specificity. Prompt employees to provide detailed reasoning for their recognition to make it more meaningful and impactful.

3. Align with company values. Tie in encouraged recognition of company values to reinforce organizational culture (that is, choosing the core value the employee demonstrated and how).

4. Provide meaningful rewards. While monetary rewards can be effective, also consider non-monetary options like extra time off, learning opportunities, or charitable donations.

5. Lead by example. Encourage leadership to actively participate in the program, demonstrating its importance and value.

6. Measure and adjust. Regularly assess the program's effectiveness through surveys and participation rates, and be willing to adapt based on feedback.

By nurturing a culture of peer-to-peer recognition, leaders can complement top-down recognition and empower employees to play an active role in shaping a positive work environment and increase their sense of community.

MAXIMIZING RECOGNITION IMPACT

Recognition programs, when implemented successfully, can have a transformative impact on morale, productivity, and engagement. However, to harness the full potential of these initiatives, organizations must adopt a strategic approach. This involves continuously measuring the program's effectiveness and maintaining flexibility to adapt. Additionally, leaders must be aware of and actively work to avoid common pitfalls that can undermine the program's success.

To truly understand the impact of your recognition efforts, it's essential to establish clear metrics and regularly assess their effectiveness. Key performance indicators (KPIs) to consider include employee engagement scores, retention rates, productivity metrics, program participation, and recognition frequency. These quantitative measures can be complemented by qualitative feedback gathered through focus groups, surveys, and regular check-ins with team members. This approach ensures your program stays in line with your goals and is meeting the needs of your team.

While it's important to assess the data related to your recognition program, it's also necessary to be aware of the most frequent challenges in implementing peer-to-peer recognition programs. Research indicates that personal bias, an unsuitable organizational culture, confusing criteria, and lack of valuable rewards are the biggest pitfalls.[16] Personal bias can skew recog-

---

16 Ho, N. S., & Nguyen, L. T. M. (2021). Challenges in the implementation of peer-to-peer recognition. *SHS Web of Conferences, 124.* https://doi.org/10.1051/shsconf/202112408007

nition with favoritism and undermine the credibility and fairness of the program. If the organization is extremely hierarchical or leaders aren't bought into the recognition efforts, the program will fail. Confusing or inconsistent criteria can lead to uncertainty about what constitutes recognition-worthy behavior and end up discouraging participation. Lastly, a lack of rewards that the team believes are valuable can eliminate the impact of recognition and cause engagement to wane.

To overcome these challenges, organizations should establish clear, objective criteria for recognition, work on cultivating a supportive culture, provide comprehensive information on the program's goals and how the process works, and make sure that recognition is accompanied by meaningful, *personalized* appreciation.

One additional challenge in leadership-driven programs is striking the right balance between frequency and intensity of recognition. Truly, recognition can be woven into daily leadership practices, from regular check-ins to goal-setting meetings that define how achievements will be recognized to performance reviews and company communications. Ideally, training on recognition techniques is included in leadership development programs. Leaders must be careful not to over-recognize, which can lessen the value of praise, but also avoid under-recognizing, which can lead to employees feeling underappreciated.

By viewing your recognition program as an ever-evolving practice and addressing these potential issues, companies can create a program where the appreciation truly resonates with employees across all generations.

FINAL THOUGHTS

Recognition, when personal and authentic, has the power to improve workplace culture and increase engagement across generations. While my research revealed some surprising insights about how different age groups prioritize recognition, the underlying need to feel valued is universal.

As relatable leaders, our challenge is to move beyond one-size-fits-all approaches and create recognition practices that resonate on an individual level. This requires curiosity, flexibility, and a willingness to change and adapt when our methods aren't as impactful as we would hope.

Remember that recognition is not a standalone leadership solution but an amplifier of other core leadership qualities like respect, trust, and clear communication. When woven together, recognition becomes part of your organizational DNA and creates an environment where all employees feel seen, valued, and inspired to reach their potential.

CONNECTION CATALYSTS

Reflect on a time when you received meaningful recognition at work. What made it impactful, and how can you apply this insight to recognize your team members?

_____

_____

_____

_____

How does your current approach to recognition align with what your team members actually value? What steps can you take to understand better and meet their individual preferences?

_____

_____

_____

_____

Consider the generational mix in your team. How might you adapt your recognition practices to resonate with both older and younger employees?

_____

_____

_____

_____

CHAPTER 7

Purpose: Aligning Intention with Impact

"Purpose is the compass that guides us, aligning our efforts with the impact we want to create."

Jessica spun in her chair at the hospital's data analytics department, rolling her eyes at yet another spreadsheet filled with endless rows of data. "Another day, another database," she muttered under her breath. The clock on Jessica's computer mocked her: 3:17 p.m. She had been at her desk for what seemed like forever, yet there were hours to go. She sighed, closing her shopping tabs and maximizing the spreadsheet she'd been avoiding all afternoon. She half-heartedly began analyzing patient data. All she saw were endless columns and faceless numbers—miles away from the life-saving mission her company talked about every staff meeting.

"Everything okay over there, Jessica?" her new team leader, Nick, asked, looking up from a nearby desk.

"Oh, I'm fine," Jessica replied with a forced smile. "Just working on the new data on wait times."

Nick paused and frowned, "Hmmm, I've learned from my teenage kids that when someone says 'Fine,' it never means they're actually fine. What's going on?"

Jessica hesitated but decided to be honest, "It's just...sometimes the data feels mindless and boring. I know you are newer on this team, but when I signed on, there was so much talk about the difference I would be making. Honestly, it feels like nothing I am doing really matters, you know?"

Nick nodded, "I get that. It's easy to lose sight of the bigger picture when you're in the weeds with data all day." He paused, then continued, "You know, I have an idea that might help put those numbers into perspective. How would you feel about shadowing some of our medical staff for a few days?"

Jessica's eyebrows raised in surprise. "Really? I could do that?" Nick nodded. "Sometimes, to do our best work, we need to step back and see the bigger picture," he explained.

Over the next few weeks, Jessica spent time away from her computer shadowing nurses during their rounds, observing doctors with their patients, and sitting in on a staff meeting for one of the cardiovascular floors. During that time, she found herself face to face with the data points she'd been analyzing—transforming columns of numbers and formulas into stories of real people whose lives were directly impacted by the numbers she worked with daily, from the predictive models she developed for improving appointment scheduling and the resource allocation recommendations made based on patient flow analysis, to the treatment effectiveness reports she generated from clinical trial data. Each example reinforced how her behind-the-scenes analytical work played a role in improving patient care and patient outcomes.

When she returned fully to her department, she found Nick at his desk and shared, "What an incredible opportunity, thank you. I have to say, I get it now." Nick smiled in reply, "You're welcome, and more importantly, I'm so happy that you see how much your work matters. I could tell you repeatedly, but it's so much more impactful to witness it."

As Jessica settled back into her work, she found herself tackling her data with a newfound perspective. The hours were still as long as the columns, but she knew that her insights could lead to real improvements in patient care. She felt more connected than ever to the hospital's mission and found her own sense of purpose through that. It made all the difference in her work.

PURPOSE: MORE THAN JUST A BUZZWORD

Jessica's experience highlights a fundamental human need that extends far beyond the walls of any hospital or office building—the need for purpose. Purpose has consistently emerged as a critical component of employee engagement, satisfaction, and the overall success of an organization. But what exactly do we mean by "purpose" in a professional context?

At its core, purpose is about understanding the "then what" of our work. As I explored in my previous book, the concept of one's "then what" is how we find meaning and direction in both our personal and professional lives. You reach the goal, but "then what?" You meet the quota, but "then what?" This simple question pushes us to look beyond our achievements and consider the larger impact of and motivation behind our efforts. It's about understanding the ripple effect of our actions and connecting our daily tasks to a greater purpose. The "then what" is the driving force behind our actions. It's the reason we do what we do, the impact we want to have, and the change we want to see in the world.

For Jessica, her "then what" wasn't just about compiling data or creating spreadsheets. It was about improving patient care, potentially saving lives, and making a real difference in patient

outcomes. Once she connected her daily tasks to this larger purpose, her entire perspective on her work changed.

This concept of "then what" isn't just for individual employees—it's for leaders as well. As a leader, understanding your own
"then what" can help you articulate an inspiring vision to and for
your team. Getting a clear picture of what drives you can provide direction for your leadership. It can help you make decisions
that align with your ultimate goals and values rather than getting
caught up in short-term distractions.

Moreover, helping your team members discover their own
"then what" within your organization can lead to increased engagement and job satisfaction. It can motivate your employees by showing
them how their individual efforts contribute to a larger, meaningful goal. When employees can see how their work aligns with
their personal values and goals, they're more likely to be committed, creative, and productive.

In the sections that follow, we'll explore practical strategies
for connecting team goals to a sense of purpose, integrating individual purpose into the organizational mission, and overcoming
common challenges in purpose-driven leadership. We'll also discover how you can help your team members discover their own
"then what" and align it with your organization's mission.

RESEARCH ON PURPOSE AND LEADERSHIP

I've always professed that human beings are hardwired for connection, which they are, but they are also hardwired for meaning.[1] Our
search for purpose is as fundamental to our nature as our need for

---

1   Baumeister, R. F., & Vohs, K. D. (2002). The pursuit of meaningfulness in
    life. In C. R. Snyder & S. J. Lopez (Eds.), *Handbook of Positive Psychology*
    (pp. 608–618). UK: Oxford University Press.

social bonds. The benefits of purpose extend far beyond fulfillment at work. Finding purpose and meaning in one's life leads to better overall well-being, higher life satisfaction, greater positive affect, and less negative affect.[2,3] With 70 percent of employees believing their sense of purpose is broadly defined by their work, it's essential to explore and define what truly drives us.[4]

Studies have consistently demonstrated the importance of purpose and meaningful work across generations in the workplace. A recent survey of more than 3,500 employees revealed that meaningful work outranked compensation, perks, and culture across all age groups.[5] Research has revealed that meaningful work yields significant benefits for both employees and organizations, including increased job satisfaction, engagement, innovation, and commitment, improved performance and productivity, and reduced absenteeism and turnover rates.[6]

2   Anglim, J., Horwood, S., Smillie, L. D., Marrero, R. J., & Wood, J. K. (2020). Predicting psychological and subjective well-being from personality: A meta-analysis. *Psychological Bulletin, 146*(4), 279–323. https://doi.org/10.1037/bul0000226

3   Pfund, G. N., Ratner, K., Allemand, M., Burrow, A. L., Hill, P.L. (2022). When the end feels near: Sense of purpose predicts well-being as a function of future time perspective. *Aging & Mental Health, 26*(6), 1178–1188. https://doi.org/10.1080/13607863.2021.1891203

4   Dhingra, N., Samo, A., Schaninger, B., & Schrimper, M. (2021, April 5). Help your employees find purpose—or watch them leave. *McKinsey & Company.* https://www.mckinsey.com/capabilities/people-and-organizational-performance/our-insights/help-your-employees-find-purpose-or-watch-them-leave

5   Workhuman. (2024, September 26). AI is so 2024. Say "hi" to Human Intelligence™.https://resources.globoforce.com/research-reports/the-future-of-work-is-human

6   Steger, M. F. (2016). Creating meaning and purpose at work. In L. G. Oades, M. F. Steger, A. D. Fave, & J. Passmore (Eds.), *The Wiley Blackwell Handbook of the Psychology of Positivity and Strengths-Based Approaches at Work* (pp. 60–81). New York, NY: John Wiley & Sons, Ltd. https://doi.org/10.1002/9781118977620.ch5

Scholars have defined three key dimensions of meaningful work:

1. Work is significant and purposeful within an organization.

2. Work aligns with and contributes to personal life.

3. Work benefits others and contributes to the greater good.[7]

These three dimensions show just how multifaceted (and daunting) connecting teams to meaningful work can be—you're not only tasked with ensuring the work is purposeful within the organization but within their personal lives and the whole of society as well. That's a tall order!

Yet, it's this all-encompassing approach that makes meaningful work so powerful. When employees feel their work checks all three boxes, the impact can be transformative—for both themselves individually and for your organization. However, achieving this ideal state of meaningful work across all levels of an organization is easier said than done. Despite leaders recognizing its importance, there's often a disconnect between how leadership perceives purpose in the workplace and how it's experienced by employees on the front lines.

While 70 percent of employees believe their sense of purpose is largely defined by their work, only a small fraction feel they're actually fulfilling that purpose in their position.[8] An impressive 85 percent of executives and upper management say they are living their purpose at work, but only 15 percent of frontline managers and employees agree.[9] This gap underscores the need for leaders

---

7   Steger, M. F., Dik, B. J., & Duffy, R. D. (2012). Measuring meaningful work: The Work and Meaning Inventory (WAMI). *Journal of Career Assessment*, *20*(3), 322–337. https://doi.org/10.1177/1069072711436160

8   Dhingra et al., 2021.

9   Ibid.

to not only articulate the purpose of a role but also to actively help their teams connect their daily work to that larger mission.

My research supports these findings and reveals a few subtle differences in how different generations perceive and value purpose at work:

> Across all generations, the statement "The mission/purpose of my company makes me feel my job is important" received high ratings, ranging from 7.22 for Gen Z to 7.62 for boomers on a ten-point scale.

> Employees throughout all generations believe leaders should connect their work to a meaningful vision and purpose. Interestingly, while leaders recognized this need, they consistently ranked its importance lower than their teams.

> Only 32.1 percent of leaders feel they are good at connecting their team's work to meaning and purpose. This perception aligns with employee feedback among boomers, who believe their leaders have a long way to go, while Gen X gives high marks in this area.

> Employees across generations want leaders who can articulate a compelling vision while also supporting their personal and professional development.

These findings highlight the importance of purpose and meaningful work across age groups but also reveal the need for leaders to tailor their approach based on generational preferences. Organizations that can effectively communicate and embody their purpose while helping employees of all ages connect their individual roles to that larger mission are likely to see significant benefits in engagement, retention, and overall performance.

ALIGNING TEAM AND INDIVIDUAL PURPOSE WITH ORGANIZATIONAL MISSION

Now that we understand the importance of purpose in the workplace and its impact on engagement and success, let's delve into the practical aspects of how relatable leaders can create this sense of purpose.

At the core, relatable leaders have three tasks: 1) share a clear organizational mission, 2) demonstrate how the employee's work fits into the larger mission, and 3) encourage employees to find personal meaning in their work, recognizing that engagement often comes from aligning individual values.

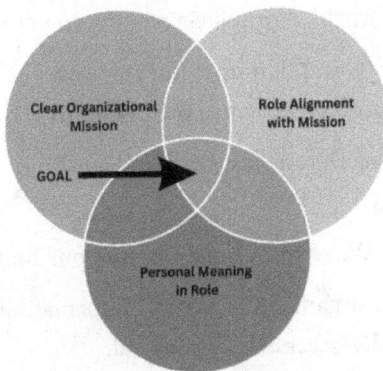

While there may be times that these three undertakings intersect naturally, there are other times when integrating these components feels like navigating a labyrinth. Let's explore strategies for tackling each.

Share a Clear Organizational Mission

A clear organizational mission serves as the North Star for a company and all who work there. It should be concise, memorable, and, in essence, be the "then what" of the organization. What is the driving force? What is its reason for being? This mission goes beyond simply stating what the company does; it encapsulates why it exists and what impact it aims to have on the world.

When crafted well, a mission statement becomes not only a motivation for employees but a tool for making decisions and part of strategy formulation. It allows organizations to prioritize and evaluate opportunities while attracting clients, partners, and teams that align with the purpose.

Here are some mission statements of well-known companies that make an impact:

Nike: To bring inspiration and innovation to every athlete in the world. If you have a body, you are an athlete.

Microsoft: Our mission is to empower every person and every organization on the planet to achieve more.

Tesla: To accelerate the world's transition to sustainable energy.

Patagonia: We're in business to save our home planet.

Google: To organize the world's information and make it universally accessible and useful.

It's important to remember that while these mission statements sound inspiring, even the most visionary companies sometimes struggle to embody their ideals fully. It doesn't negate the value of their missions, but it highlights how challenging it is to align daily operations with an overarching purpose.

For many businesses, a more practical mission statement can be just as effective. Your organization's mission might be as straightforward as "To provide the best customer service in our industry" or "To offer affordable, quality products to our local community." The key is that it accurately reflects your company's core purpose, reminds your team of why their jobs matter, and resonates with customers. Ideally, the mission statement also ties into how the organization's work positively impacts society or your community—which helps employees meet Steger's third dimension, "Work benefits others and contributes to the greater good."

If your organization lacks a clear mission statement, creating one is the first step in purpose-driven leadership. Here's a quick process you can use to begin to craft an impactful mission statement:

1. Gather input. Involve employees at all levels to collect diverse perspectives on what teams believe the organization's purpose is.

2. Define your core. Identify what your organization does, who it serves, and why what it does matters.

3. Keep it concise. Aim for a single sentence that's memorable and inspiring.

4. Make it actionable. Ensure the statement is capable of guiding decision-making and operations.

5. Test and refine. Share drafts with your teams and customers and refine them based on feedback.

Remember, this can be a work in progress. Many organizations go through several iterations of a mission statement before settling on one, and even then, they go on to change it after a time. It's okay to be malleable.

The goal is to create a mission statement that inspires both employees and customers while clearly defining your organization's unique value proposition. Once you have that mission statement? It's time for the three Cs—make sure it is consistently communicated, completely understood, and consciously embodied—from the C-suite to the front line.

Demonstrate Alignment between Individual Roles and the Organizational Mission

The second step to align your team with the company's mission is bridging the gap between day-to-day tasks and organizational purpose. While this can also be a challenge for leaders, demonstrating this alignment is how employees are able to witness and recognize how their work contributes to the bigger picture. Here are some strategies you can utilize as a leader to make that leap easier:

1. Clearly communicate job-mission connections. Explain to each employee how their specific responsibilities tie into organizational goals. Example: A manager explains to a customer service representative how their interactions directly impact customer retention, which supports the company's mission of providing exceptional service.

2. Incorporate organizational objectives into roles. When defining or updating job descriptions, write them to reflect how the job supports the goals of the organization. Example: "Contribute to monthly security innovation brainstorming sessions" added to the job description for a developer at a cybersecurity firm.

3. Provide aligned skill development. Offer training and professional growth opportunities that build the skills needed to advance the mission of the organization. Example: A hospital with a mission to provide compassionate, patient-centered care provides empathy training to all staff.

4. Share success stories. Regularly highlight examples of how individual or team efforts have worked to further the organizational mission. Example: A non-profit focused on education highlights how a grant writer's successful application led to funding for ten new after-school programs directly related to its mission of expanding educational opportunities.

5. Connect individual roles to societal impact. Help employees understand how their specific work ultimately contributes to the organization's positive impact on society or the world. Example: Show a finance team member how their work in managing budgets allows the company to invest in sustainable practices that benefit the environment.

When leaders actively assist employees in aligning their personal purpose with organizational goals, they demonstrate a profound level of respect for each individual's unique values, aspirations, and definitions of meaningful work. This approach not only acknowledges the diverse motivations within the team but also illustrates how employees' day-to-day contributions directly connect to the organization's mission and purpose. By consistently employing these strategies, leaders cultivate an environment where employees can see the impact of their work, enhancing engagement and commitment to the collective vision.

Encourage Personal Meaning in Work

Aligning purpose with personal meaning can be one of the most challenging aspects of leadership, as the driving force behind personal meaning is something that is unique to each individual. While it's essential to communicate a clear organizational mission and demonstrate how each role contributes to that mission, effective leaders must also prioritize helping employees discover their own sense of purpose within their work. As Steger's second dimension of meaningful work emphasizes, "work aligns with and contributes to personal life"—understanding how one's work fulfills personal meaning is required to improve engagement and satisfaction.

To foster this alignment between work and personal life, leaders can employ several strategies:

1. Facilitate individual purpose discovery. Organize sessions where employees can explore their personal values, strengths, and goals. Help them articulate their own "then what" and see how it aligns with their role and the organization's mission. Example: A quarterly "Purpose Mapping" workshop where employees create visual representations of their personal and professional goals.

2. Establish mentorship programs. Pair employees with mentors who can help them navigate their career path within the organization with a focus on personal goals and fulfillment. Example: A mentorship program involving senior leaders meets monthly with paired employees to discuss their career goals within the company and how they tie into personal objectives.

3. Provide opportunities for impact sharing. Create ways for employees to share how their work makes a differ-

ence—personally and through the organization. Example: A monthly "Impact Spotlight" where employees present projects they're proud of and how they've grown through the experience.

4. Encourage work–life integration. Support employees in finding ways to blend their personal passions with their work. Example: Allow time for volunteer work that is related to the company's mission.

By implementing these strategies, employees can find and grow the connection between personal meaning and their work. It's important to remember that this process is ongoing and highly individual. What brings meaning to one employee may not resonate with another, so flexibility and personalization are key.

Aligning team and individual purpose with the organizational mission is not easy, but by sharing a clear organizational mission, demonstrating how individual roles contribute to that mission, and encouraging personal meaning in work, leaders can create a purpose-driven culture that resonates across all levels of the organization and throughout all generations. In facilitating meaning, leaders create a workplace where employees aren't just working for a paycheck; they're working for a purpose that aligns with their own values and aspirations.

OVERCOMING CHALLENGES IN CULTIVATING PURPOSE

Emma could not have been more excited to take on a leadership role at the financial services firm she had worked at since she graduated from college six years ago. During that time, she worked hard and developed a well-earned reputation for her dedication and ability to get things done. When the opportunity arose to become a team leader, she jumped at the chance. She knew the team, understood their strengths, and was aware of areas with room for growth—one of which was how cynical everyone was—especially around change and new initiatives.

On her first day as team lead, Emma walked into the office with an almost naive sense of hope and determination, given her background. She was focused on reinfusing purpose into their roles. "It's time to do things differently. We're at a crossroads," Emma began, her voice steady. "We've always performed well, but I *know* we can do better. Much better. And it starts with a shift in perspective. We need to stop seeing ourselves as number crunchers and start seeing how we directly impact our client's financial futures."

As she stood in front of her colleagues, they listened politely, but she saw the skeptical glances and heard the quiet whispers. She knew they were nowhere near convinced when she caught the eye rolls. Some of the more vocal team members, like David, whom she had worked with for years, didn't bother hiding their doubts. "We've heard this before," he muttered, just loud enough for her to hear.

Emma paused, taking a deep breath. She tried to get a handle on whether she was dealing with indifference or whether it had shifted into hostility. "I get it," she said, "change is hard, and promises are cheap. But I'm not here to make promises. I'm here to ask for a chance. A chance to show you that there's a different way of working, a way that I believe is far more fulfilling—for all of us. Let me prove you wrong."

Her words hung in the air; she caught a few more doubting looks, but the eye rolls slowed. Still, she knew it was going to be an uphill battle. Over the next few weeks, Emma focused on small, tangible actions to demonstrate her commitment to change. She started by scheduling one-on-one meetings with each team member, actively listening to their frustrations and ideas. She made a point of acknowledging their past experiences with failed initiatives and validated their suspicions while gently urging them to remain open-minded.

In team meetings, Emma began sharing client success stories, connecting the team's work to positive outcomes in people's lives. She also implemented a "purpose of the week" initiative, where team members would take turns sharing how their work that week had made a difference. Yes, the eye rolls returned at first, but soon, it began to create a competition around who had the best story.

The energy started to shift. The cynicism gave way to what could only be seen as the embers of excitement.

Six months into her new role, Emma looked around at her team during a meeting. After the meeting wrapped up, David approached Emma. "You know," he said, a hint of a smile on his face, "I never thought I'd say this, but you were right. I don't know how you did it, but how I think about my work has changed."

It hadn't been easy, and there were challenges ahead, but Emma successfully navigated one of the biggest hurdles in cultivating purpose—overcoming deep-seated doubt and cynicism. By consistently demonstrating her commitment, connecting work to real-world impact, and celebrating small wins, she transformed a team that was checked out into one that genuinely appreciated the purpose of their work.

Emma's story illustrates a common challenge many leaders face when trying to reignite purpose within their teams.

The benefits of purpose-driven leadership are clear, but implementation can be difficult. Leaders can be faced with skeptics (like Emma experienced), waning dedication in difficult times, the innate challenge of balancing the needs of their organization with individual purposes, and personal purpose uncertainty among team members.

Let's explore the key challenges leaders face when cultivating purpose and how to address them effectively:

Overcoming skepticism and cynicism. There are many employees who view a mission statement or purpose as corporate jargon or simply a marketing ploy to woo customers or employees. Like Emma, leaders must lead by example and remain consistent in decisions and actions. Transparency is key, and if team members express their skepticism openly, use it as an opportunity to begin a dialogue that addresses their concerns head-on. Additionally, consistently demonstrating through actions that support the words of the mission builds trust and buy-in over time.

Maintaining a sense of purpose during difficult times. It's easy to buy into the big picture and mission when the coffers are overflowing, but teams can lose sight when facing a crisis or when adversity strikes. During these challenging times, leaders can play a pivotal role in rekindling team purpose by communicating the team's contribution to the organization's core values, sharing stories of past successes after tough times, and providing opportunities for team members to be involved in solutions and decision-making. In fact, showing commitment to the mission becomes even more critical during difficult times and can create stability and inspiration when other aspects of work feel uncertain.

Balancing individual purpose with organizational needs. Sometimes, an employee's sense of purpose doesn't precisely align with organizational goals. In these situations, leaders should work with employees to find common ground, identifying areas where personal and organizational purposes overlap. Helping employees see how their work indirectly supports aspects of the organization that align with their purpose can broaden perspectives. However, if there's a significant misalignment, honest conversations about whether the organization is the right fit long-term may be necessary.

Personal purpose uncertainty. While organizations typically have a defined purpose, one of the biggest concerns I hear from audience members after a keynote is that they are unsure of their purpose, their "then what." This is where my concept of *"return on intention"* could be helpful. Rather than pressuring employees to define their purpose for a lifetime, leaders can encourage them to set intentions for shorter periods—a quarter, a year, or even just for a specific project. This method allows for flexibility and allows employees to find meaning in their work while remaining open to evolving goals. By focusing on "return on intention," leaders can help team members align their immediate efforts with both personal growth and organizational objectives, creating a sense of purpose that's both meaningful and achievable in the near term.

Remember, cultivating a purpose-driven culture is an ongoing process that requires patience, consistency, and, most of all, adaptability. There will be setbacks and frustrations along the way, but by being aware of and proactively addressing these challenges, leaders can create a more resilient, purposeful organization. A truly purpose-driven organization is worth the effort.

MEASURING THE IMPACT OF PURPOSE-DRIVEN LEADERSHIP

As with any leadership approach, measuring the impact of purpose-driven initiatives is required. We know that organizations that support the integration of purpose and meaning in one's work leads to increased job satisfaction, engagement, innovation, and commitment, as well as increased productivity, but how do we gauge the success of our efforts? Even though purpose may seem more intangible, there are ways to assess effectiveness, including:

1. Purpose alignment surveys: Conduct regular surveys to assess how well employees understand and connect with the organization's purpose. These surveys can include questions about how employees see their work contributing to the larger mission and whether they feel their personal values align with the organization's purpose. (The survey at the end of this book also includes a section on example questions relating to purpose.)

2. Qualitative feedback: Conduct one-on-one interviews and group discussions to collect data about how purpose is being integrated throughout the organization. These can also be incorporated into performance reviews.

3. Decision-making audit: Regularly audit critical decisions to make sure they are made in alignment with the organization's mission. This can help ensure that purpose truly guides organizational strategy and operations.

4. Purpose case studies: Regularly document where your organization's purpose-driven approach led to positive outcomes. These case studies can provide concrete examples of impact and serve as inspiration for your teams.

Measuring the impact of purpose-driven leadership doesn't only justify the investment of time and money but also allows organizations to evolve and improve their programs. Be prepared to adjust your measurement approach as you learn what works best for your organization. By regularly assessing the integration and impact of purpose in your organization, you can ensure that your purpose-driven leadership approach remains effective, authentic, and aligned with both organizational goals and employee needs. This data-driven approach, combined with a genuine commitment to purpose, can help create a truly thriving, purpose-driven organization.

FINAL THOUGHTS

Purpose is not just a lofty ideal—it's a fundamental driver of the success of your team. As relatable leaders, we have the opportunity and responsibility to connect our teams to a sense of purpose that aligns individual passions with organizational mission. This requires articulating a clear vision, demonstrating how each role contributes to that vision, and helping employees discover personal meaning in their work.

While cultivating purpose presents challenges and a requirement of energy that can feel overwhelming at times, the impact is undeniable. Purpose-driven organizations see increased innovation, retention, and overall success. By consistently reinforcing purpose, we can create cultures where employees don't just work for a paycheck but for goals they believe in.

CONNECTION CATALYSTS

Reflect on a time when you felt a strong sense of purpose in your work. What contributed to that feeling, and how can you create a similar experience for your team?

_____

_____

_____

_____

Identify one way you can better communicate how your team's daily tasks connect to the larger organizational mission this week.

_____

_____

_____

_____

Schedule brief "purpose check-ins" with two to three team members to discuss how they find meaning in their roles and brainstorm ways to enhance that connection.

PART FOUR

TRANSPIRE

CHAPTER 8

Motivation: Channeling Passion into Progress

"True leaders ignite their own fire, but cast enough sparks to light the way for their team."

Imagine a leader who is not only motivated themselves but also motivating to their team—a leader who can nurture the drive and ambitions of their team, and someone who has an internal passion and translates that passion into inspiring others. This isn't just a pipe dream; it's what relatable leaders can achieve when they master the art of motivation. Motivation is the fuel that drives individuals and teams to achieve their goals. It's the invisible force that transforms potential into performance, ideas into innovation, and challenges into opportunities.

A highly motivated workforce drives both engagement and productivity and leads to a significant boost in the company's overall performance.[1] Motivated employees are more efficient in and more satisfied with their roles.[2] While employees seek lead-

---

1   Uka, A., & Prendi, A. (2021). Motivation as an indicator of performance and productivity from the perspective of employees. *Management & Marketing, 16*(3), 268–285. https://doi.org/10.2478/mmcks-2021-0016

2   Paais, M., & Pattiruhu, J. R. (2020). Effect of motivation, leadership, and organizational culture on satisfaction and employee performance. *Journal of Asian Finance, Economics and Business, 7*(8), 577–588. https://doi.org/10.13106/jafeb.2020.vol7.no8.577

ers who are motivating, we cannot overlook the importance of a leader's own drive—"motivated" is the number nine trait overall in terms of what makes a relatable leader, with millennials ranking it as one of the top five traits.

There is a clear need for relatable leaders who both feel motivated and can unlock motivation within their employees. In Chapter 8, we'll explore how relatable leaders can cultivate motivation—in both themselves and within their teams. To fully grasp motivation, relatable leaders must understand motivation— its psychological foundation, the need for extrinsic and intrinsic motivators, and how motivation changes by generation.

UNDERSTANDING MOTIVATION

Motivation is the driving force behind human behavior, influencing not just what we do but how we do it. In the workplace, understanding motivation allows leaders to help both themselves and their teams reach their full potential. Several theories have emerged over the years that provide valuable insights into what drives people and provide a foundation for our understanding of motivation. Let's explore some of the most influential theories that have shaped our understanding of motivation in the workplace.

Key Theories of Motivation

1. Maslow's Hierarchy of Needs

    Abraham Maslow's theory suggests that human needs are arranged in a hierarchy, from basic physical needs to self-actualization.[3] Maslow's theory encourages leaders to

---

3   Maslow, A. (1959). *New Knowledge in Human Values*. New York: Harper & Row.

ensure basic needs (like job security and compensation) are met before moving on to higher-level motivators like recognition and personal growth.

2. Self-Determination Theory

Developed by Richard Ryan and Edward Deci, self-determination theory proposes that humans are motivated by three innate psychological needs: autonomy (the ability to make choices), competence (the feeling of being effective), and relatedness (the desire to connect with others).[4]

3. Expectancy Theory

Expectancy theory, developed by Victor Vroom, claims that employee motivation is driven by three main factors: expectancy (the belief that effort will lead to a desired performance), instrumentality (the belief that performance will result in a specific reward), and valence (the value placed on those rewards). In sum, the theory maintains that individuals are motivated to maximize the benefits they gain from their work by believing their efforts will be recognized and rewarded.[5]

4. Equity Theory

Proposed by John Stacey Adams, this theory suggests that employees are driven by a sense of fairness, balancing their contributions and rewards against those of their peers to maintain equity. When individuals perceive an

4   Deci, E., & Ryan, R. (1985). *Intrinsic Motivation and Self-Determination in Human Behavior.* New York: Plenum Press.

5   Buford, J. A., & Lindner, J. R. (2002). *Human Resource Management in Local Government: Concepts and Applications for HRM Students and Practitioners.* Nashville, TN: South-Western College Publishing.

imbalance, they may adjust their efforts, seek changes in rewards, or even leave the organization to restore their sense of fairness.[6]

5. Goal-Setting Theory

Developed by Edwin Locke, this theory states that clear, challenging, and attainable goals, coupled with feedback, are primary drivers of employee motivation and performance.[7] The theory emphasizes that specific and challenging goals lead to higher performance than vague or easy goals.

These are just a handful of the most prevalent psychological theories on motivation, as there are at least twenty to twenty-five widely recognized motivation theories (not including variations). The key is to select and apply different theories based on needs, context, and team dynamics. For instance, Maslow's hierarchy reminds us to address basic needs before moving on to higher-level motivators. Self-Determination Theory highlights the importance of giving employees autonomy and opportunities for growth. Expectancy Theory emphasizes the need for clear associations between effort and rewards, while Equity Theory stresses the importance of fairness in our recognition programs. Finally, the Goal-Setting Theory informs how we structure objectives and provide feedback. Leaders can create a motivational strategy that works for their teams by pulling from the theories that best apply.

---

6   Adams, J. S. (1965). Inequity in social change. In L. Berkowitz (Ed.), *Advances in Experimental Social Psychology*, vol. 2 (pp. 267–299). San Diego, CA: Academic Press, Inc.

7   Locke, E. A. (1980). Latham versus Komaki: A tale of two paradigms. *Journal of Applied Psychology*, 65(1), 16–23. https://doi.org/10.1037/0021-9010.65.1.16

Now that we have a basic understanding of the theories behind motivation, we need to understand the forms of motivation that influence employee behavior before moving into the practical application of motivation.

Extrinsic vs. Intrinsic Motivation

Motivation can be categorized into two types: extrinsic and intrinsic. Understanding the differences between these types of motivation and when to utilize each kind will allow leaders to choose how to best inspire their teams.

Extrinsic motivation is related to behaviors driven by external rewards or pressures. Extrinsic motivators include monetary benefits like bonuses and salary increases, promotions, and title upgrades. It also involve avoiding negative consequences like criticism.[8]

Intrinsic motivation is primarily psychological and comes from within the individual. Intrinsic rewards in the workplace span from being proud of one's work and respect from peers to personal growth, increased trust from managers, enjoyment of tasks, feelings of accomplishment, skill development, project autonomy, and team collaboration.[9]

Underlying effective motivational strategies is a fundamental respect for employees' individual needs, desires, and potential. When leaders take the time to understand what truly drives each team member, they're showing respect for their unique perspectives and aspirations. The goal for leaders is to find a balance

8   Madsen, S. R., & Wilson, I. (2008). The influence of Maslow's humanistic views on an employee's motivation to learn. *Journal of Applied Management and Entrepreneurship, 12*(2), 46–62.

9   Manzoor, F., Wei, L., & Asif, M. (2021). Intrinsic rewards and employee's performance with the mediating mechanism of employee's motivation. *Frontiers in Psychology, 12.* https://doi.org/10.3389/fpsyg.2021.563070

between both types of motivation. Relying primarily on extrinsic motivators can undermine intrinsic motivation.[10] This is known as the "overjustification effect"—a phenomenon where introducing external rewards for a behavior that was already intrinsically motivated can reduce the intrinsic motivation for that behavior.[11] For example, offering a bonus for a project an employee already enjoys might actually *decrease* their intrinsic motivation to perform.

In contrast, focusing entirely on intrinsic motivation without consideration for external factors fails to account for the interplay between the two. Research shows that the most effective approach combines both types of motivation, using extrinsic rewards while also focusing on intrinsic motivation.[12] For example, a project that challenges an ambitious employee (intrinsic motivation through skill development) might be paired with a bonus upon successful completion (extrinsic motivation). Or a promotion (extrinsic) might come with increased autonomy over one's work (intrinsic). The key for relatable leaders is to understand how these motivators interplay and to create an environment where both external rewards and internal drivers are present and aligned.

Let's explore how leaders can leverage both types of motivation.

---

10 Rey-Biel, P., Gneezy, U., & Meier, S. (2011). When and why incentives (don't) work to modify behavior. *Journal of Economic Perspectives, 25*(4), 191–210. https://www.researchgate.net/publication/227359671_When_and_Why_Incentives_Don't_Work_to_Modify_Behavior

11 Peters, K. P., & Vollmer, T. R. (2014). Evaluations of the overjustification effect. *Journal of Behavioral Education, 23,* 201–220. https://doi.org/10.1007/s10864-013-9193-1

12 Conrad, D., Ghosh, A., & Isaacson, M. (2015). Employee motivation factors: A comparative study of the perceptions between physicians and physician leaders. *International Journal of Public Leadership, 11*(2), 92–106. https://doi.org/10.1108/ijpl-01-2015-0005

Extrinsic motivators

Extrinsic motivators play a significant role in employee engagement and satisfaction. Relatable leaders need to understand how to effectively use these external rewards to drive performance without undermining intrinsic motivation.

Monetary rewards

Monetary rewards, that is, salaries, bonuses, and profit-sharing, are the primary extrinsic motivators. They fulfill basic needs by providing financial security and tangible recognition of an employee's value. However, their motivational impact can be short-lived—once the rewards are depleted or employees reach a comfortable level of financial security, motivation dwindles.[13]

Best practices for monetary rewards:

- Ensure fairness and transparency in compensation structures.
- Tie monetary rewards to specific performance goals or metrics.
- Offer a mix of short-term (sales competitions, quarterly bonuses) and long-term incentives (stock options, deferred compensation).
- Regularly review and adjust compensation to remain competitive in your industry.
- Provide clear communication about how rewards are determined and disbursed.

Example: A sales team receives quarterly bonuses based on exceeding target quotas.

---

13 Manzoor, Wei, & Asif, 2021.

Promotions and career advancement

Growth and advancement opportunities provide powerful extrinsic motivators while tapping into intrinsic drives. Extrinsically, they offer tangible rewards such as higher salaries, new titles, and increased organizational status.

My research highlights the importance of growth and advancement opportunities in motivating employees. When asked to rank factors that inspire them, respondents overwhelmingly selected "Employees are motivated when leaders empower their growth and advancement" as the most important. This finding is even more significant when paired with another discovery—employees identified this area as where leaders have the most room for improvement, while leaders ranked themselves highest here. This disconnect reveals a critical area for leadership development and focus.

Best practices for leveraging the extrinsic aspects of career advancement:

- Establish clear, objective criteria for promotions.
- Create and communicate transparent career paths within the organization.
- Ensure promotions come with appropriate increases in compensation and benefits.
- Provide visible recognition of advancement through new titles or responsibilities.
- Regularly review and adjust advancement opportunities to remain competitive.

Example: A retail chain provides management training programs for high-performing floor staff.

Recognition and rewards programs

Recognition and rewards programs, as explored in Chapter 6, are strong extrinsic motivators that can significantly impact employee engagement and performance. They provide tangible and intangible acknowledgment of an employee's contributions to the organization. However, their effectiveness can vary based on factors such as timing, authenticity, and individual preferences. When designing recognition programs, remember that personalization and authenticity are vital to making employees feel genuinely valued.

Best practices for recognition and rewards programs:

- Personalize recognition of individual preferences and generational differences.
- Ensure recognition is timely, specific, and authentic to maximize impact.
- Implement a mix of formal (awards, bonuses) and informal (verbal praise, thank-you notes) recognition.
- Encourage peer-to-peer recognition alongside top-down recognition.
- Align recognition with company values and goals to reinforce desired behaviors.
- Regularly evaluate and update programs based on employee feedback and changing needs.

Example: An engineering firm allows peers to nominate colleagues for awards at monthly all-hands meetings.

As we've explored, extrinsic motivators play a significant role in employee engagement and satisfaction. However, to create a truly motivated and committed workforce, relatable leaders must also tap into intrinsic motivators.

Intrinsic motivators

Intrinsic motivators can have an even more lasting impact on employee engagement and satisfaction. Intrinsic motivation is related to internal drive and taps into an employee's personal values, interests, and sense of purpose. They can lead to deeper commitment and higher quality work over time.

Relatable leaders who can effectively harness these intrinsic motivators create a situation where employees are not just working for a paycheck or a promotion but because they find genuine fulfillment and meaning in their work as individuals. This intrinsic motivation can lead to increased creativity, problem-solving, and overall job satisfaction.

Let's explore three key intrinsic motivators: autonomy, skill development, and purpose and meaning.

Autonomy

Autonomy in the workplace refers to how much freedom and control employees have over their work. The greater flexibility fosters a sense of ownership and responsibility. Research has shown that employees with a high sense of autonomy have higher job satisfaction and overall well-being.[14]

Best practices for increasing autonomy:

- Allow flexible work arrangements where possible (flexible hours, remote work options).
- Provide clear goals and expectations, but allow employees to decide how to achieve them.
- Create opportunities for independent projects and initiatives.
- Encourage independent thinking and innovation.

---

14   University of Birmingham. (2017, April 24). Autonomy in the workplace has positive effects on well-being and job satisfaction, study finds. *ScienceDaily*. https://www.sciencedaily.com/releases/2017/04/170424215501.htm

Example: A tech company adopts a "20 percent time" policy where employees can work on passion projects one day a week.

Skills development

While growth and advancement offer extrinsic rewards, they also powerfully tap into intrinsic motivation through the opportunity for skills development. This intrinsic aspect focuses on employees' desire for personal progress and evolution.

Continuous learning and skills improvement are powerful intrinsic motivators. They provide a sense of personal achievement, increased confidence, and alignment with individual goals for self-improvement.

Best practices for nurturing the intrinsic aspects of growth and skills development:

- Offer diverse training and development opportunities, both formal and informal.
- Create challenging assignments that challenge abilities.
- Provide resources for self-directed learning.
- Recognize and celebrate the development of new skills.
- Create a culture that values continuous improvement and learning.

Example: A law firm provides an annual learning stipend for employees to use on courses or conferences of their choice.

Purpose and meaning

As we discussed in Chapter 7, employees who have a sense of purpose are significantly more motivated and engaged. When people understand how their work contributes to the larger goals of the organization, they're more likely to be invested in their roles.

Best practices for cultivating purpose and meaning:

- Clearly communicate the organization's mission, vision, and values.
- Regularly share stories of how the organization's work impacts customers and the community.
- Help employees understand how their individual roles contribute to larger goals.
- Encourage employees to articulate their own sense of purpose and how it aligns with their work.

Example: A non-profit organizes field trips for office staff to see their work's impact firsthand.

As stated previously, the best motivation balances both extrinsic and intrinsic factors. While extrinsic motivators like monetary compensation, promotions, and recognition drive short-term performance improvements, intrinsic motivators like autonomy, skill development, and a sense of purpose create long-lasting engagement and commitment. Relatable leaders understand that motivation requires flexibility and individualization. The idea is to offer a range of motivational drivers, allowing employees to connect with what resonates best.

Generational Differences in Motivation Preferences

Relatable leaders must also recognize that preferences around motivation are not the same across all generations of employees. While individual differences always come before generational stereotypes, my research into relatable leadership has uncovered some fascinating insights into how motivational preferences vary across generations.

Here's a chart below providing a quick guide to generational differences in motivation.[15,16,17]

Baby Boomer	Gen X	Millennial	Gen Z
Raises and promotions	Monetary rewards	Monetary rewards	Mentorship
Position of authority	Work-life balance	Purpose and meaningful work	Purpose and meaningful work
Mentorship opportunities	Autonomy	Feedback and skills training	Feedback
Acknowledgment	Opportunities for skill advancement	Flexibility	Diversity

Relatable leaders can use this information as a general guide, but the goal is always to understand individual motivators. For example, while Gen Z generally values mentorship, some may prioritize autonomy. Regular check-ins and open dialogues about what drives each team member can help leaders tailor their moti-

15 Glass, A. (2007). Understanding generational differences for competitive success. *Industrial and Commercial Training*, *39*(2), 98–103. https://doi.org/10.1108/00197850710732424

16 Ballone, C. (2007). Consulting your clients to leverage the multi-generational workforce. *Journal of Practical Consulting*, *2*, 9–15. https://www.researchgate.net/publication/228477964_Consulting_your_clients_to_leverage_the_multi-generational_workforce

17 Gurchiek, K. (2016, May 9). What motivates your workers? It depends on their generation. *SHRM*. https://www.shrm.org/topics-tools/news/inclusion-diversity/motivates-workers-depends-generation

vational approaches effectively. The key is to create a motivational strategy that's diverse enough to appeal to all generations while still allowing for personalization.

By understanding both the psychological foundations of motivation and the generational differences in motivational preferences, relatable leaders can craft more effective strategies to inspire and engage their multigenerational teams.

In addition to generational differences, leaders face an additional challenge: motivating entire teams composed of diverse individuals. Motivating teams as a whole is oftentimes more complicated than motivating individuals due to the varying beliefs, values, goals, and expectations within the group.[18] Leaders must find ways to inspire and engage the team while still acknowledging individual needs and preferences.

This reality underscores the importance of a flexible, multifaceted approach to motivation. As we explore specific motivational strategies in the following sections, remember that the most effective leaders balance team unity with individual recognition and empowerment.

THE LEADER'S ROLE IN MOTIVATION— MOTIVATING SELF

David stared blankly at the sales figures on his screen. They were good—better than last quarter even—but he felt nothing. No excitement, no sense of accomplishment. Just...emptiness. He glanced at his watch: 6:15 p.m. Another day gone, blurring into the rest.

---

18   Clark, R. E. (2005). Research-tested team motivation strategies. *Performance Improvement, 44*(1), 13–16. http://dx.doi.org/10.1002/pfi.4140440107

A knock interrupted his thoughts. "David? You got a minute?" Sarah, his assistant sales manager, stood in the doorway.

"What is it?" he replied, his tone flat.

Sarah took a beat before stepping in, "This is not easy for me to share, but I have to tell you. The team's been talking. They're worried about you—they think you seem...off."

David shrugged. "We're hitting our targets, aren't we? What else matters?"

"The numbers are fine," Sarah agreed, "but there's more to it than that. Everyone feeds off your energy. Right now, it feels like all you're doing is going through the motions."

Her directness caught David off guard. He leaned back, the tension in his shoulders becoming far more noticeable. "What do you suggest?"

"There's this leadership workshop next week. It's supposed to be good for stress management, team motivation, and mindset. Maybe it's worth a shot?"

David rolled his eyes. "Some woo-woo nonsense? It's not going to change our quarterly goal."

"No," Sarah agreed, "but it could change *you*."

David flinched, "Ouch. Fine. I'll look into it. But I'm not drinking the Kool-Aid."

Begrudgingly, David signed up for the workshop. It wasn't filled with magical solutions, but something began to shift as he listened to other leaders share similar struggles.

During a break, he found himself chatting with Carmen, another sales director. "You know," she said, sipping her coffee, "I used to think being tough was the only way to lead. But I was just creating a team of stressed-out clones."

David nodded, recognizing his own approach in her words. "What changed?"

Carmen smiled wryly. "I realized that my own lack of energy was infecting my entire team. It wasn't about being tough or soft—we hear all of this talk about engaging teams, but I was so far from being engaged myself."

David frowned. "What do you mean?"

"Think about it," Carmen explained. "When was the last time you felt genuinely excited about a sale? Or psyched about your team's accomplishment?" David paused for far too long.

"If *you* can't remember, how can you expect your team to feel that way?"

Her words hit home. David realized he'd been so focused on numbers that he'd lost sight of why he loved his job in the first place.

Back at the office the following week, David was more aware. He started small—taking a moment each morning to remind himself why he got into sales leadership in the first place. It wasn't about the software itself but the challenge of handling complex deals and the satisfaction of solving challenging business problems for clients.

In their next team meeting, David paused instead of diving straight into numbers. "Before we start, I want to hear about your wins this week. Big or small."

The team seemed surprised, but slowly, stories started to emerge. A difficult client finally signing on. A creative solution to a logistics problem.

Over the next few weeks, David made a conscious effort to reconnect. He started joining his reps on more client calls, not to micromanage but to remember the thrill of closing a deal. He initiated a weekly "lessons learned" session where the team could share both successes and failures openly.

A month later, Sarah knocked on his door again. "Have you seen the latest numbers?"

David nodded, a small smile playing on his lips. "They're up. Not drastically, but it's a good trend."

"It's not just the numbers," Sarah pointed out. "The team... they seem different. More engaged. Like you. Whatever you're doing, keep it up. It's making a difference."

As she left, David turned back to his computer. The pressure was still there, but it felt different now. Instead of a weight, it felt more like excitement around the next challenge to tackle. David realized that by rekindling his own motivation, he'd started to reignite the spark in his entire team.

David's story highlights an often-overlooked aspect of motivation—the leader's motivation. As mentioned at the start of this chapter, my research found that "motivated" is the number nine trait overall in terms of what creates a relatable leader. Millennials rank it even higher as a top five trait. As leaders, the ability to stay self-motivated is directly correlated to motivating and inspiring one's team. During a recent keynote at a tech industry conference, an audience member approached me with a story similar to David's. This reinforced my belief that leader motivation is a universal challenge, transcending industry boundaries.

For leaders to effectively motivate themselves (and, by extension, their team), it's necessary to focus on three areas:

1. Set clear goals.

2. Align work with personal values.

3. Maintain work–life balance.

Set Clear Goals

Clear goals provide direction and purpose, which are fundamental to maintaining motivation. When leaders have well-defined objectives for themselves, it becomes easier to focus energy and stay on track. To effectively use goals for self-motivation:

- Set both short-term and long-term goals for yourself.
- Ensure goals are SMART (specific, measurable, achievable, relevant, time-bound).[19]

  - Specific: Clearly define what you want to accomplish.

  - Measurable: Include concrete criteria to measure progress.

  - Achievable: Set realistic and attainable goals.

  - Relevant: Align goals with your leadership vision and organizational objectives.

  - Time-bound: Set a specific timeframe for achieving the goal.

- Regularly review and adjust your goals as needed.
- Celebrate achievements for positive motivation.

Clear SMART goals provide direction and purpose, allowing leaders to measure progress and stay focused. Research has shown that leaders with strong self-regulation and the ability to manage and control their thoughts, emotions, and behaviors are

---

19 Bovend'Eerdt, T. J., Botell, R. E., & Wade, D. T. (2009). Writing SMART rehabilitation goals and achieving goal attainment scaling: A practical guide. *Clinical Rehabilitation, 23*(4), 352–361. https://doi.org/10.1177/0269215508101741

more effective in sustaining motivation, especially in relation to goal setting.[20]

Align Work with Personal Values

For leaders, aligning work with personal values creates a strong foundation for motivation and purpose. When their actions reflect their core beliefs, they inspire trust and commitment within their teams. To better align your work with your values:

- Reflect on your core values.
- Identify how elements of your work connect with and support these values.
- Create ways to incorporate your values into your leadership style.
- Communicate the importance of values alignment to your team.

As we have repeatedly seen, motivation is deeply connected to how well our work aligns with personal values. Leaders who find a connection between their career and their beliefs experience improved performance, stronger employee engagement, more effective decision-making, and better organizational outcomes overall.[21] This intrinsic motivation can help leaders to overcome challenges and stay resilient during difficult times.

20   Steinmann, B., Klug, H. J. P., & Maier, G. W. (2018). The path is the goal: How transformational leaders enhance followers' job attitudes and proactive behavior. *Frontiers in Psychology, 9.* https://doi.org/10.3389/fpsyg.2018.02338

21   Črešnar, R., & Nedelko, Z. (2020). Understanding Future leaders: How are personal values of generations Y and Z tailored to leadership in industry 4.0? *Sustainability, 12*(11), 4417. https://doi.org/10.3390/su12114417

Maintain Work–Life Balance

A sustained level of motivation cannot exist without balancing one's personal life and work. Research has shown that if you want to be an effective leader, it is essential to leave work at work.[22] A study out of the University of Florida studied teams throughout the United States and found that when leaders could disconnect from work at home, they were more energized, connected, and effective the next day. A well-balanced life contributes significantly to sustained motivation and prevents burnout.

To maintain a healthy work-life balance:

- Set boundaries between work and personal time.
- Prioritize self-care and personal relationships.
- Encourage a culture of balance within your team.
- Delegate and empower team members.

Staying motivated as a leader is the only way to support and motivate a team. By setting clear goals, aligning your values with your work, and maintaining a healthy work-life balance, you can avoid your own burnout and ensure both your success and the success of your employees.

LEADER'S SELF-MOTIVATION CHECKLIST

Rate yourself on a scale of one to four for each item (1 = Strongly Disagree, 4 = Strongly Agree)

---

22 Klug, K., Felfe, J., & Krick, A. (2022). Does self-care make you a better leader? A multisource study linking leader self-care to health-oriented leadership, employee self-care, and health. *International Journal of Environmental Research and Public Health, 19*(11), 6733. https://doi.org/10.3390/ijerph19116733

	1	2	3	4
I have clear, achievable goals for myself	1	2	3	4
My work aligns with my personal values	1	2	3	4
I maintain a healthy work–life balance	1	2	3	4
I celebrate my own achievements, big and small	1	2	3	4
I regularly seek new challenges and learning opportunities	1	2	3	4
I have strategies to manage stress and avoid burnout	1	2	3	4
I connect regularly with mentors or peers for support	1	2	3	4
I can articulate my purpose as a leader	1	2	3	4
I take time to reflect on and renew my motivation	1	2	3	4

Total Score: _____ / 36

Scoring Guide:
- 31–36: Highly self-motivated
- 21–30: Good motivation, room for improvement
- 11–20: Need to focus on self-motivation strategies
- Below 11: Immediate attention is required to avoid burnout

BURNOUT: THE BIGGEST BARRIER TO MOTIVATION

We've spent quite some time on how to build motivation within a team, but it's equally important for relatable leaders to be aware of its counterpart: burnout. Imagine developing the perfect motivation strategy, only to have it completely fall apart because we overlooked something as critical as employee well-being. Overwhelming pressure and stress can exhaust even the most motivated employees, leading to a state that undermines all previous motivational efforts. Understanding, preventing, and addressing burnout is essential to any comprehensive motivation strategy. By staying attuned to the signs of burnout and taking proactive steps to maintain a healthy working environment, leaders can make sure their motivational initiatives are not wasted.

Burnout has been defined as "a work-related state of exhaustion that occurs among employees, which is characterized by extreme tiredness, reduced ability to regulate cognitive and emotional processes, and mental distancing."[23] The consequences of burnout are emotional, physical, and intellectual. Burnt-out employees have low job satisfaction, low engagement, increased absenteeism, and are 2.6 times more likely to be searching for a new job.[24,25]

---

23 Otto, M. C. B., Van Ruysseveldt, J., Hoefsmit, N., & Van Dam, K. (2020). The development of a proactive burnout prevention inventory: How employees can contribute to reduce burnout risks. *International Journal of Environmental Research and Public Health, 17*(5), 1711. https://doi.org/10.3390/ijerph17051711

24 Salvagioni, D. A. J., Melanda, F. N., Mesas, A. E., González, A. D., Gabani, F. L., & De Andrade, S. M. (2017). Physical, psychological and occupational consequences of job burnout: A systematic review of prospective studies. *PLoS ONE, 12*(10). https://doi.org/10.1371/journal.pone.0185781

25 Gallup, Inc. (2023, August 2). Employee burnout: The causes and cures. *Gallup.* https://www.gallup.com/workplace/508898/employee-burnout-causes-cures.aspx

Burnout is also an expensive mistake. Gallup found that burned-out employees can cost $3,400 for every $10,000 in salary because of their lack of productivity.[26] And the expense to replace an employee? That's one-half to two times their annual salary.[27] To avoid allowing burnout among your teams, leaders must work to prevent it in the first place.

Recognizing Burnout

Prevention of burnout requires an understanding of the signs. The Maslach Burnout Inventory (MBI) is one of the most widely used scales to measure burnout.[28] The scientifically proven (and copyrighted—hence why sharing specific questions is prohibited) scale was developed for several professions and included a version for general professionals. The scale focuses on assessing three areas—emotional exhaustion, cynicism, and professional efficacy.[29] Emotional exhaustion is defined as feelings of being emotionally depleted, cynicism is characterized as indifference and attachment to one's job, and professional efficacy involves feelings of lack of competence and ability to do one's job.[30]

While the MBI provides a detailed and research-backed method for measuring burnout, leaders can also recognize burn-

26 PCBB. (2022, March 30). Mitigating employee stress for higher productivity. *PCBB*. https://www.pcbb.com/bid/2022-03-30-mitigating-employee-stress-for-higher-productivity
27 Ibid.
28 Maslach, C., & Jackson, S. E. (1981). The measurement of experienced burnout. *Journal of Organizational Behavior, 2*(2), 99–113. https://doi.org/10.1002/job.4030020205
29 Ibid.
30 Maslach, C. (2003). Job burnout: New directions in research and intervention. *Current Directions in Psychological Science, 12*(5), 189–192. https://doi.org/10.1111/1467-8721.01258

out through practical, day-to-day observations. Here are behaviors to look out for:

- Changes in behavior and attitude: Negative shifts in demeanor, including becoming withdrawn, visibly stressed, or irritable.
- Emotional exhaustion: Fatigue, decreased energy, feelings of being overwhelmed, and frustration.
- Complacency and detachment: Indifference or negative attitudes toward work, colleagues, or the organization as a whole.
- Reduced competence: Struggling with previously manageable tasks and productivity and work quality declines.
- Increased absenteeism: Increase in frequency of sick days or arriving late to work.

Preventing Burnout

As explored in earlier chapters on communication, trust, recognition, and motivation, the steps to preventing burnout are deeply intertwined with many of the core principles of relatable leadership. Here are six strategies to protect your team (and yourself) from burnout before it starts:

1. Encourage work–life balance. Promote a culture where employees take regular breaks, use their PTO, and are able to disconnect after hours.

2. Set clear and realistic expectations. Make sure that the goals and deadlines set are attainable. Check-in if you're unsure, and make adjustments as necessary.

3. Promote autonomy. Give employees a sense of control by allowing them to have a say in how they complete their work.

4. Provide support and resources. Offer mental health resources and make sure that your culture is one where seeking help is not only normalized but encouraged.

5. Foster respect. Cultivate an atmosphere of respect and collaboration. As discussed at the start of this book, feeling valued and respected is the foundation of employee happiness.

6. Encourage open communication. Ensure employees are comfortable discussing their challenges and stressors. Regular one-on-one meetings provide a safe space for employees to voice concerns before they become overwhelming.

Burnout Recovery

What happens when your team is already showing the symptoms of burnout? When burnout has already set in, immediate action is required. If one or more of your team members appear burnt out, the first step is to acknowledge and validate them and their current state. Beginning the conversation with something like: "It seems like you are dealing with a lot right now. I know the work has been stressful, and I want to talk about how we can support you and make it more manageable." The goal is to open the lines of communication and let them know you are aware of the situation and are committed to their support.

Secondly, the employee needs time to recover. Encourage them to take time off to rest. Support healthy habits if possible—one organization I have worked with offers yoga three times a week in the office. Additionally, consider providing flexible work arrangements or resources such as counseling or coaching to further promote well-being. Most importantly, when they return, evaluate their workload. Work with them to determine what needs to be delegated and what can remain. Without a change in workload, burnout becomes a continuous cycle.

Burnout is a serious and *expensive* leadership challenge that can profoundly affect both employees and organizations. By taking a multidimensional approach—focusing on recognizing, preventing, and addressing burnout—leaders can protect their teams and organizations from its impact.

FINAL THOUGHTS

Motivation is what transforms your team's potential into actual performance. As we've explored in this chapter, cultivating motivation—both in yourself and your team—is a complex but required task for relatable leaders. Understanding the key theories of motivation, the nuances of extrinsic and intrinsic motivators, and generational differences in preferences allows for a personalized approach to recognizing your team.

As a leader, please do not forget that prioritizing your own motivation is just as important—you are and will always remain an enormous influence on your team's ambitions and commitment. Your energy and enthusiasm (or lack thereof) will directly impact their drive and morale.

Remember, motivation isn't a one-time campaign, it needs to become an ongoing program with consistent application and continuous adaptation. As you move forward, continue to reflect on your motivational strategies, seek feedback, and be willing to adjust your approach. The effort you put into cultivating motivation will pay dividends in team performance, satisfaction, and overall organizational success. In the end, relatable leaders who can effectively motivate themselves and their teams are those who will truly inspire progress and achieve remarkable results.

CONNECTION CATALYSTS

Reflect on your own motivational drivers. How have they changed over your career? How might understanding these changes help you better motivate your team?

_____

_____

_____

_____

Review your current reward and recognition programs. How could you adjust them to better balance extrinsic and intrinsic motivation?

_____

_____

_____

_____

Consider an employee who seems disengaged. What intrinsic motivators might resonate with them based on what you know about their values and goals?

_____

_____

_____

_____

CHAPTER 9

Unlocking Potential: Facilitating Team Growth

"Don't just manage jobs; manage potential."

Emily was buzzing with frenetic energy. "This could be incredible," she excitedly shared with her manager. She continued, "This new approach could reduce production costs by 20 percent and speed up our delivery times by at least a week. I've run the numbers and even did a small test. The results were incredible!"

Her manager, Ram, glanced up from his computer, his expression a mix of disinterest and skepticism. "That's interesting, Emily. But we have established processes for a reason. Changes like this need to go through proper channels," he dismissively replied.

Emily took a deep breath, refusing to allow Ram's response to completely dim her enthusiasm. "Of course, I get that, but if you could just take a look at the data, I'm sure you'd see the potential."

Ram hesitated for a moment, then shrugged. "Look, Emily, you're great, but this isn't your job. We have R&D teams for this sort of thing. By the way, do you have that report that I asked for? Those numbers won't crunch themselves."

Months passed, with Emily's idea gathering dust. She watched as competitors began to implement ideas similar to her concept and saw them gaining market share. Frustrated and feeling undervalued,

Emily made a difficult decision. She resigned, taking her expertise and ideas with her. Within a year, she had launched her own startup, built around the very idea her former company had dismissed.

Two years later, Emily's company had become a major disruptor in the industry. Her former employer scrambled to catch up, realizing far too late the value of the innovation they dismissed.

Emily's story is a reminder of what can happen when an organization overlooks the potential within its team. As relatable leaders, one of our most significant responsibilities is to nurture and develop the full potential of our employees. By recognizing, developing, and investing in the potential of our teams, we not only advance their individual goals, we also strengthen the organization as a whole. Unlocking the potential of your team goes beyond assigning responsibilities and performance reviews, it's about empowering employees to contribute ideas, push their limits, take on challenges, and continue to evolve.

THE CASE FOR EMPLOYEE GROWTH

Studies consistently show that organizations prioritizing employee development see higher engagement, productivity, and innovation levels. A Gallup survey reveals that investing in employee development leads to 11 percent increased profits and doubles the likelihood of retaining employees.[1] Gallup also found that when employees know and use their strengths, they are six times more engaged and have higher performance.[2]

As we've discussed throughout this book, employees across generations have differing expectations of leaders and organiza-

1   DeSimone, R. (2019, December 12). Improve work performance with a focus on employee development. *Gallup.* https://www.gallup.com/work place/269405/high-performance-workplaces-differently.aspx

2   Ibid.

tions, yet *all* generations agree in their desire for professional development.[3] For younger employees, particularly Gen Zs and millennials, career growth and advancement aren't just important—they are often the primary reason for staying with an organization.[4] However, this need for development is not unique to younger generations.

In fact, growth opportunities are a significant factor in employee retention for all generations. Employees are far less likely to leave their jobs when they see a path for development within their roles. "Career growth opportunities" consistently rank as the top factor driving people to change jobs, regardless of age.[5] Employees who make an internal move up have a 75 percent retention rate at the two-year mark, while those who don't make such a move have only a 56 percent chance of staying with the company.[6]

Even with the clear benefits of encouraging advancement and the risks of neglecting employee potential, many organizations fall short in this area. Alarmingly, over a third of employees feel underutilized at work.[7] There has been so much attention focused (deservedly so) on the challenges caused by burnout, but

3   Brower, T. (2022, August 28). What the generations want from work: New data offers surprises. *Forbes*. https://www.forbes.com/sites/tracybrower/2022/08/28/what-the-generations-want-from-work-new-data-offers-surprises/

4   De Smet, A., Mugayar-Baldocchi, M., Reich, A., & Schaninger, B. (2023, April 20). Gen what? Debunking age-based myths about worker preferences. McKinsey & Company. https://www.mckinsey.com/capabilities/people-and-organizational-performance/our-insights/gen-what-debunking-age-based-myths-about-worker-preferences

5   DeSimone, 2019.

6   LinkedIn Learning. (n.d.). 2024 Workplace Learning Report. *LinkedIn Learning*. https://learning.linkedin.com/resources/workplace-learning-report

7   Andrus, D. (2021, March 8). One-third of employees feel underutilized at work. *ALM Benefits Pro*. https://www.benefitspro.com/2021/03/08/one-third-of-employees-feel-underutilized-at-work/?slreturn=20241008104447

boreout can be equally damaging to both morale and productivity.[8] Boreout occurs when employees are under-stimulated and lacking in meaningful challenges. Employees suffering from boreout are dissatisfied and disengaged and in desperate need of a chance to grow.

My research reveals a significant disconnect between employees' desire for growth and what they perceive as opportunities for development. As discussed in Chapter 8, this gap is particularly notable when we compare how leaders and employees view growth opportunities. Employees are hungry for growth and advancement opportunities, ranking it as the top factor that inspires them at work. However, this same area was identified by employees as the one where leaders have the most room for improvement, while leaders saw themselves as performing well in this domain.

To bridge this gap and foster growth within their teams, leaders must not only provide opportunities for promotion but also create an environment that encourages new ideas and innovation. This involves empowering employees to experiment, take risks, and bring fresh perspectives to their roles. Encouraging innovation can drive continuous improvement and make work far more engaging and fulfilling—both personally and professionally.

The most effective leaders will be those who can facilitate their teams' desire for growth and advancement while encouraging an innovative culture. In this chapter, we'll explore practical frameworks and strategies for unlocking the full potential of your team members. By embracing these approaches, relatable lead-

---

8   Jessurun, J. H., Weggeman, M. C. D. P., Anthonio, G. G., & Gelper, S. E. C. (2020). Theoretical reflections on the underutilization of employee talents in the workplace and the consequences. *Sage Open*, *10*(3). https://doi.org/10.1177/2158244020938703

ers can create empowered teams where every member feels supported in reaching their full potential and contributing innovative solutions to the organization.

UNDERSTANDING EMPLOYEE POTENTIAL

Employee potential refers to an individual's ability to grow, develop, and perform within an organization. As relatable leaders, we are responsible for nurturing that potential within our teams, but what exactly do we mean by "potential," how can we spot it, and how can we effectively develop it? Let's explore.

Potential is a multifaceted concept, from identifying high-potential employees to recognizing the capabilities of every team member. While we can sometimes focus on our standout performers, relatable leaders understand that *all* employees have potential to grow. By expanding how we look at potential, we can create avenues for all our teams to advance. Larger organizations may contain talent management in-house, where they have dedicated teams and sophisticated methods for identifying and developing potential, including assessments and analytics. However, all leaders can effectively assess potential looking at a few key areas:

- Ability to learn and apply new skills
- Capacity for leadership and influence
- Adaptability to change and new challenges
- Innovative thinking and problem-solving capabilities
- Emotional intelligence and interpersonal skills

When assessing potential, it's helpful to have a framework to guide your observations. The following checklist can help to evaluate these five areas of employee potential and help you gain insights into your team:

Key Area	Assessment Questions
Ability to learn and apply new skills	~ Do they actively seek opportunities to learn? ~ How quickly does the employee grasp and apply new concepts? ~ Do they learn from their mistakes and make improvements?
Capacity for leadership and influence	~ Can they inspire and motivate others? ~ Do they take initiative in leading projects or teams? ~ How well do they handle responsibility and decision-making? ~ Are they respected and trusted by their peers?
Adaptability to change and new challenges	~ How do they handle unexpected challenges? ~ Are they comfortable stepping outside their comfort zone? ~ Can they quickly adjust to new priorities or demands? ~ Do they maintain a positive attitude during change?
Innovative thinking and problem-solving capabilities	~ Do they bring new ideas to the table? ~ Can they effectively solve complex problems? ~ How creative are they in finding solutions? ~ Do they approach problems with a strategic mindset?

Emotional intelligence and interpersonal skills	~ How well do they understand and manage their emotions?
	~ Do they build strong, positive relationships?
	~ How well do they handle conflict or challenging conversations?
	~ Are they empathetic and considerate of others' feelings?

It's important to note that this checklist is nowhere near exhaustive. Many of these traits, if absent, can be taught and developed. Remember, potential is not just about what an employee can do now but what they could achieve with the proper support and opportunities.

Cognitive Diversity as a Competitive Edge

When assessing potential, it's also essential to recognize and value neurodiversity within your team. Neurodivergent employees are those whose brains process information differently from the typical or "neurotypical" person.[9] These individuals may have conditions such as autism spectrum disorder, ADHD, dyslexia, or other neurological differences.[10] By embracing these differences, you unlock unique strengths that neurodivergent employees bring to the table, particularly in areas such as cognitive functioning, comprehension, and creativity.[11]

These neurodivergent traits can translate into exceptional workplace capabilities:

9   Cleveland Clinic. (2022, June 2). *Neurodivergent.* Cleveland Clinic. https://my.clevelandclinic.org/health/symptoms/23154-neurodivergent

10   Neurodivergent. (2024). *Merriam-Webster Dictionary.* https://www.merriam-webster.com/dictionary/neurodivergent

11   Doyle, 2020.

- Problem-solving: Unique perspectives often lead to novel solutions.
- Creativity: Divergent thinking can spark innovation and fresh ideas.
- Hyperfocus: The ability to concentrate intensely on tasks of interest.
- Pattern recognition: Identifying trends and connections others might miss.
- Attention to detail: Spotting discrepancies or errors that others overlook.

By recognizing and nurturing these strengths, leaders can unlock tremendous potential within their teams. It's important to create an environment that supports neurodivergent employees, providing accommodations where needed and ensuring an atmosphere where they feel accepted and appreciated for diverse thinking styles. Remember, neurodiversity is not a limitation but a valuable form of cognitive diversity that can drive organizational success when properly understood and leveraged.

Understanding and assessing employee potential is just the first step. The real challenge lies in nurturing and developing that potential.

CREATING A CULTURE OF GROWTH AND INNOVATION

Regardless of neurotype, a workplace focused on growth and innovation is about more than just encouraging new ideas—it's a complete shift in how organizations view challenges and opportunities. At the heart of growth at work is the concept of a growth mindset. Coined by psychologist Carol Dweck, a growth mindset is the belief that abilities can be developed through effort and learning—challenges are seen as opportunities.[12] This is in direct contrast with a fixed mindset, which is the belief that abilities are unchangeable and challenges may be avoided due to fear of failure.[13]

As highlighted earlier, a relatable leader views employee potential not just in their current abilities but what an employee could achieve with the right support and opportunities—a true growth mindset. Recall Emily's story—had her company embraced this culture of growth and innovation, they might have benefited from her ingenuity rather than losing her and her ideas.

Relatable leaders can utilize several strategies to promote a culture of growth and innovation, including the following:

1. Lead by example. Promoting a growth mindset within a team starts at the top. Relatable leaders must model a willingness to learn, adapt, and view challenges as opportunities for growth.

2. Encourage experimentation. Create an atmosphere that encourages employees to express new ideas and try new things without fear.

3. Recognize and reward innovation. Implement recognition programs that celebrate both successes and attempts.

4. Promote cross-functional collaboration. Break down silos and encourage teams from different departments to work together.

---

12   Dweck, C. S. (2017). *Mindset: Changing the Way You Think to Fulfill Your Potential.* London: Hachette UK Limited.
13   Ibid.

5. Foster psychological safety. Create an environment where team members feel comfortable expressing ideas, asking questions, and admitting mistakes without fear of judgment, as explored in Chapter 3.

6. Encourage stepping out of comfort zones. Push employees to take on new challenges and responsibilities that stretch their abilities.

7. Provide constructive feedback. Offer timely, specific, and actionable feedback that helps employees learn and improve.

Innovation in Action

There are many organizations that are doing innovation right and creating an atmosphere where new ideas and growth thrive. Here are a handful of real-world examples of organizations nurturing creativity, encouraging experimentation, and promoting a growth mindset.

Google's 20 Percent Time—Google's famous "20 percent time" policy allows employees to dedicate 20 percent of their hours to side projects of their choosing. This decision has paid dividends, as it has led to the development of products like Gmail, Google News, and AdSense.

3M's 15 Percent Rule—Since 1940, 3M has allowed employees to spend 15 percent of their time working on their own projects. This has led to breakthrough products like Post-it Notes and Scotch Tape.

Novartis's Genesis Labs—Pharmaceutical company Novartis launched an internal startup program called

Genesis Labs to encourage innovation. The program invites employees to submit "crazy, transformative ideas" for reimagining medicine, creating a safe space for bold thinking and cross-functional collaboration.

Pixar's Braintrust—Pixar Animation Studios has developed "Braintrust" meetings—sessions to encourage candid feedback on works-in-progress. The meetings have been touted as being responsible for the successful development of movies like *Toy Story* and *Finding Nemo*.

Don't forget you do not have to lead a Fortune 100 company to encourage an environment where growth and innovation thrive. Relatable leaders can cultivate an atmosphere that nurtures development and encourages creative thinking regardless of size.

A culture with a growth mindset sets the stage for employee development. However, it is equally important to provide concrete opportunities for professional development. Let's explore various types of opportunities and how relatable leaders can effectively implement them within their teams.

PROFESSIONAL DEVELOPMENT OPPORTUNITIES

Professional development is a vital component of unlocking employee potential and encouraging growth. Professional development is defined as cultivating an employee's growth within the company, guided by both organizational needs and the employee's capabilities, achievements, and preferences.[14]

---

14 Armstrong, M., & Taylor, S. (2020). *Armstrong's Handbook of Human Resource Management Practice*, 15th ed. London: Kogan Page Ltd.

There are several types of professional development that an organization can offer their employees, with some of the primary options including:

- Mentorship programs
- Conferences/workshops/seminars
- Courses (certificate to degree)

Let's begin with one of the most effective ways to nurture potential, which is through mentorship programs.

Mentorship Programs

The word "mentor" has its origins in ancient Greek literature, Homer's *The Odyssey*. In the poem, King Odysseus relies on his friend Mentor to guide his son Telemachus through life. When Mentor fails to live up to his name, the goddess Athena disguises herself as Mentor to guide Telemachus. The word has evolved since then to mean a more experienced individual guiding us through life. In professional contexts, mentors are typically more senior team members who provide guidance, support, and knowledge to less experienced colleagues.

Mentorship has been associated with several positive outcomes in the workplace, including positive attitudes, job satisfaction, organizational and job commitment, and career success for the mentee.[15,16] The benefits go both ways as well, as mentors have been found to gain new insights and perspectives, as well

15 Baranik, L. E., Roling, E. A., & Eby, L. T. (2010). Why does mentoring work? The role of perceived organizational support. *Journal of Vocational Behavior, 76*(3), 366–373. https://doi.org/10.1016/j.jvb.2009.07.004

16 Ivey, G. W., & Dupré, K. E. (2020). Workplace mentorship: A critical review. *Journal of Career Development, 49*(3), 714–729. https://doi.org/10.1177/0894845320957737

as increase their self-esteem, self-development, and satisfaction.[17] This reciprocal nature can create a powerful cycle that improves workplace dynamics for all involved. However, even though 76 percent of people recognize the value of mentors, only 37 percent actually have one.[18]

Given the significant benefits, implementing an effective mentorship program can be a foundational strategy for nurturing employee potential. Designing a successful mentorship program requires considerable thought and planning. Here is an example flow of developing a mentorship program:

Step 1: Create a Matching Process

Determine whether your matching process will either allow mentees to choose a mentor or pair mentors and mentees. The matching should be based on personalities, goals, interests, mentoring styles, and/or backgrounds. A survey or questionnaire can help gather the data needed to assess compatibility. A word of caution: Finding the right fit between mentee and mentor is essential, as a negative experience can be detrimental. Research has shown that a negative mentoring relationship can lead to turnover, stress, and lower productivity.[19] Be mindful of parings and allow for flexibility if there isn't a fit.

Step 2: Define Expectations and Structure

Once matches are made, the next step is to establish clear expectations and provide structure to mentoring relation-

17 Ward, W. L., Love, J., & Williams, V. N. (n.d.). Mentoring. *AAMC.* https://www.aamc.org/professional-development/affinity-groups/gfa/mentoring

18 Comaford, C. (2019, July 5). 76% of people think mentors are important, but only 37% have one. *Forbes.* https://www.forbes.com/sites/christinecomaford/2019/07/03/new-study-76-of-people-think-mentors-are-important-but-only-37-have-one/

19 Ivey & Dupré, 2020.

ships. This can be done through an orientation (in person or virtual) or materials that outline goals, expected time commitment, and guidelines for communicating. A typical schedule has mentors and mentees meeting monthly. To ensure focused and productive conversations, it's helpful to define topics such as career planning and advancement, work-life balance, skills development (for example, research, teaching, leadership), and networking for visibility. In some organizations, mentors are provided training prior to the start of the relationship to set them up for success and cover potential issues like confidentiality, boundaries, and bias.

Step 3: Check-In and Recognize

Regularly evaluate and recognize mentors and mentees. Create a method for gathering feedback on the relationship and the program, and have more extensive reviews quarterly or biannually. The insights can be used to continue to develop the program. Equally important is acknowledging the time and effort invested. Recognize mentors for their contributions (review Chapter 6 for ideas) and celebrate mentee growth. Know that throughout this process, the mentor/mentee relationship may shift into colleagues and collaborators. Be open to mentees seeking new mentors as their career progresses and provide guidance on how to gracefully conclude or transition mentoring relationships.

Step 4: Measure Outcomes

Lastly, to demonstrate the value of your mentorship program and continue to improve it, we need to collect data—both quantitative (for example, retention rates, promotion statistics) as well as qualitative feedback (personal and professional growth, well-being, and career satisfaction). Sharing case studies of successful mentor/mentee relationships can highlight the program's impact and encourage others to participate.

These steps will provide the parameters for a successful mentorship, yet it can be even more helpful to learn from the examples of successful mentorship programs in action. If you are looking for additional inspiration, look at the organizations that have developed successful mentorship programs, including Mastercard, Caterpillar, General Electric, and Microsoft. While these companies are massive, the core of their programs can be adapted to an organization of any size. Whether you run a small team or a large enterprise, creating a successful mentorship program is achievable by matching thoughtfully, setting expectations, checking in often, and measuring results.

While mentorship programs can be invaluable to employee growth, they are just one component of a complete professional development strategy. Another element is providing opportunities for employees to expand their knowledge and network through conferences, workshops, and seminars.

Conferences/Workshops/Seminars

Equipping teams with new skills and industry insights through conferences, workshops, and seminars has been found to significantly boost employee satisfaction, productivity, and retention.[20] These events not only create opportunities to learn but also facil-

---

20 Tharenou, P., Saks, A. M., & Moore, C. (2007). A review and critique of research on training and organizational-level outcomes. *Human Resource Management Review, 17*(3), 251–273. https://doi.org/10.1016/j. hrmr.2007.07.004

itate networking with colleagues and peers. Each of these formats provides something different and can be utilized to meet particular objectives.

Conferences, both external and internal, provide a multifaceted experience for employees. External industry events, whether association-based or held by private entities, offer opportunities to learn about the latest trends and innovations while networking with peers and industry leaders. Internal conferences, on the other hand, facilitate knowledge sharing within the organization, fostering cross-departmental collaboration and alignment. Both types of conferences can inspire employees with new ideas, providing a more comprehensive view of the industry and the company's place within it. Attending these events can spark innovation, broaden perspectives, and energize teams with fresh insights.

Workshops offer a more focused, hands-on learning experience. Unlike conferences, which tend to be more passive in nature, workshops involve active engagement where the audience participates in practical exercises, masterminds, and skill-building activities. Workshops are ideal for developing specific competencies, whether they are technical skills related to their tasks or soft skills like leadership and communication. For organizations looking to take their team's growth to the next level, my consulting company, The Magnet Method, offers tailored workshops designed to engage, inspire, and equip employees with the tools they need to excel in areas of communication, leadership, emotional intelligence, and building authentic connections.

Seminars are a middle ground between conferences and workshops, typically focusing on a specific topic but in a more lecture-based format than workshops. They often feature subject matter experts who delve deep into a particular area and are usually offered for professionals in fields such as legal, financial, medical, and educational sectors. Seminars focus on providing in-depth knowledge and updates on industry-specific trends, regulations, and best practices.

If you are looking to offer conferences, workshops, or seminar programs as part of your professional development program, the options should be tailored to the employee and matched to organizational goals for the greatest return on investment. It is also important to create a fair and equitable process for determining who attends events, set clear expectations and processes for sharing knowledge with colleagues post-event, and track ROI through post-event surveys.

Courses (Certificate to Degree)

Another potential professional development offering is tuition assistance or reimbursement to give employees the opportunity to advance their education, from certificate programs to full degrees. Certification options include industry-specific programs, technical skills training, and leadership and management courses. Full degree programs include MBAs and specialized master's degrees. While costly, these types of educational opportunities can provide significant benefits, including increasing employee retention, job performance, and talent attraction.[21]

Organizations should follow key best practices when rolling out a course program, including:

---

21 Gonzalez, E. (2024, May 10). 5 benefits of offering tuition reimbursement. *The Motley Fool.* https://web.archive.org/web/20240710162337/https://www.fool.com/the-ascent/small-business/human-resources/tuition-reimbursement/

- Clearly defined eligibility and application processes to ensure fairness and transparency
- Aligning offerings with organizational goals to maximize the benefit
- Consider a contractual commitment post-completion/graduation to ensure ROI

Companies of all sizes, from small businesses to large corporations, have successfully implemented tuition assistance programs as a valuable employee benefit. However, one consequential factor to consider when offering these programs is the tax implications. The Internal Revenue Service (IRS) allows students only up to a certain amount in tuition reimbursements tax-free each year, with the excess amount being subject to income tax. Many companies either cap the benefit at the IRS limit or pay the educational institutions directly.

With a blend of mentorship, workshops, and/or courses, organizations can create a professional development program that is beneficial to both the employees and the organization.

OVERCOMING CHALLENGES IN THE DEVELOPMENT OF POTENTIAL

While nurturing employee potential is a critical component of an organization's success, there are many challenges leaders face throughout the process.

Resource Constraints

One of the most common challenges in employee development is the limitation of resources—both financially and in terms of time. Organizations are often challenged to allocate enough funds for training and education. In these situations, creativity is key. How can you utilize internal expertise for training? Are there low-cost online resources?

An additional resource constraint is the energy and time it takes to implement professional development. Leaders who are already overworked may find that adding mentoring or coaching would stretch them beyond the brink. Self-awareness and self-preservation are key—ensure leaders are aware of their limitations and are provided flexibility in workload distribution based on goals.

Managing Expectations and Timelines

Expectations are the root of all frustrations, and when the expectations between employees and their organization are misaligned, it can lead to a strained work environment. Employees may have unrealistic expectations about their level of influence, career progression, and development opportunities. Organizations and leaders may have unrealistic expectations around employee skill development or return on investment.

To address this, leaders need to encourage open and transparent communication around all elements of employee development and set clear and attainable goals.

Balancing Individual Growth with Team Needs

Another significant challenge is the balance between fostering individual employee growth and the needs of their team and the organization as a whole. While we need to invest in each team member's potential, leaders must also consider the employees' current responsibilities. This balancing act can be particularly challenging when development activities take time away from their day-to-day responsibilities or when individual growth goals don't align perfectly with the needs of the team.

Overcoming Leader's Ego and Fear

Perhaps one of the most overlooked challenges in potential development is the leader's own ego and fear. Some leaders may feel threatened by the growth of their team members, fearing that they might be outshone or replaced. This can lead to unconscious (or sometimes conscious) efforts to limit employee growth opportunities.[22] Overcoming this requires self-awareness and an understanding that their success as a leader is measured by the growth and success of their team. Embracing vulnerability, being open to learning alongside their team, and viewing employee growth as a reflection of their own leadership success can help leaders overcome these internal barriers.

FINAL THOUGHTS

Unlocking the potential of your team is a non-negotiable strategy to compete in today's marketplace. As we've discussed throughout this chapter, nurturing employee growth is both desired and expected by all generations. The good news is that it pays dividends, from increased engagement and productivity to improved retention and innovation.

Creating an authentic culture of growth and innovation requires a multifaceted approach. It starts with recognizing the potential in all employees and maintaining a growth mindset, knowing that all team members have the ability to grow

22   Basran, J., Pires, C., Matos, M., McEwan, K., & Gilbert, P. (2019). Styles of leadership, fears of compassion, and competing to avoid inferiority. *Frontiers in Psychology*, 9. https://doi.org/10.3389/fpsyg.2018.02460

and evolve with the right support and opportunities. By creating options for professional development that fit your organization— from mentorship and workshops to educational opportunities— you provide your employees with the tools they need to reach their potential.

As relatable leaders, our role is to create an environment where every team member feels empowered to grow, take risks, and bring their best selves to work each day. The challenges in this process are real, from resource constraints to managing expectations. However, by approaching these obstacles with creativity, open communication, and a commitment to your team, we can create genuinely transformative opportunities for our teams.

CONNECTION CATALYSTS

Reflect on your professional growth journey. What experiences or opportunities had the most significant impact? How can you create similar experiences for your team?

_____

_____

_____

_____

Identify one team member whose potential you feel is underutilized. Schedule a one-on-one meeting to discuss their aspirations and brainstorm ways to align their growth with organizational needs.

_____

_____

_____

_____

Challenge yourself and your team to learn one new skill this month that's outside your usual scope. Share progress and insights in team meetings.

_____

_____

_____

_____

CHAPTER 10

Eliminating Hurdles: How Leaders Clear the Path

"Don't just clear the path; teach your team to climb."

In writing this book, I've repeatedly thought to myself, "Leadership is a LOT of work. It is filled with responsibility, demands, and conflicting opinions. You feel pulled in every direction, exhausted by the pressure and expectations." As you are aware, ALL of this is true. Leadership can be exhausting and stressful, yet I also know that through these challenges are opportunities for growth, both for yourself and your team.

This chapter is about how leaders will continue to be tested—through the inevitable obstacles they will face and the consistent evolution of the role of a leader. The path to success is rarely without bumps. From communication breakdowns to organizational silos, from the challenges of remote work to the struggle to maintain motivation during difficult times, leaders face numerous potential roadblocks. However, none of these hurdles are insurmountable. All can be approached as opportunities for growth with the right mindset and strategies. In the pages to come, we'll explore practical approaches to overcoming these obstacles, drawing on research, real-world examples, and the principles of relatable leadership we've discussed throughout this book. By the end of this chapter, you'll be equipped to handle anything that comes your way.

OVERCOMING COMMON COMMUNICATION PITFALLS

Clear and effective communication, as we explored in Chapter 5, is a cornerstone of relatable leadership. Yet, even with the best intentions, leaders will encounter communication pitfalls that can undermine their efforts to connect, communicate, and inspire. One of the most pressing issues is dealing with difficult conversations.

Navigating Difficult Conversations

Leaders are no strangers to challenging conversations. From providing constructive feedback and addressing performance issues to mediating conflicts and delivering tough news that impacts morale, these interactions are an inevitable part of leadership. These conversations can be emotionally charged and, if not handled well, can negatively impact engagement and team dynamics. Engaging in constructive conversations enhances well-being, strengthens connections, and boosts productivity.[1] Difficult conversations can yield the same positive results when held in a supportive environment.[2]

---

1   Reis, H. T. (2017). The interpersonal process model of intimacy: Maintaining intimacy through self-disclosure and responsiveness. In J. Fitzgerald (Ed.), *Foundations for Couples' Therapy: Research for the Real World* (pp. 216–225). UK: Routledge.

2   Tjosvold, D., Wong, A. S., & Yi-Feng, N. C. (2014). Constructively managing conflicts in organizations. *Annual Review of Organizational Psychology and Organizational Behavior, 1*(1), 545–568. https://doi.org/10.1146/annurev-orgpsych-031413-091306

My research revealed interesting generational and gender differences as they relate to one's comfort level with difficult conversations. Younger generations generally felt more at ease engaging in these challenging interactions, while women and Gen X/ boomer supervisors reported feeling less comfortable. However, regardless of demographic, mastering these conversations is necessary for both relatable leaders and their teams.

To help navigate these choppy waters, I've developed a three-step framework called the "Me-You-We" approach to difficult conversations and situations. This approach aligns with the principles of authentic and respectful leadership we've explored throughout this book and provides a structured and thoughtful approach to conversations. Let's dive into each step:

Me: The first step involves self-awareness and self-reflection. Before engaging in a difficult conversation, leaders should take time to understand their own emotions, thoughts, and goals. Ask yourself: How do I feel at this moment? How do I feel about this situation? Am I feeling an emotion (anger, frustration, sadness) that may interfere with the conversation? This introspection helps ensure that you approach the conversation calmly and confidently.

You: The second step focuses on empathy and understanding the other person's perspective. Consider how they might feel about the situation and the information they may have. By putting yourself in their shoes, you're more likely to approach the conversation with respect and consideration.

We: The final step involves creating a goal for the resolution of the situation. What is the "we"? What is the ideal outcome of the situation? How can you set the optimal resolution as the North Star that guides your conversation? In doing so, the words and tone you choose will reflect your intention and likely the outcome.

Example: A team leader needs to address a consistently underperforming employee.

Me: The leader reflects on their feelings about the situation. They recognize frustration but are also concerned about the employee's well-being. They remind themselves that the goal is improvement, not punishment.

You: The leader considers the employee's perspective. Are there personal issues affecting their work? Do they understand performance expectations? Are they struggling with specific elements of a project?

We: The leader sets a goal for the conversation: to create a plan for improvement that addresses concerns and supports the employee's success.

Conversation: "I've noticed some challenges with your recent work (Me: calm, factual). I'd like to understand your perspective on this (You: showing empathy). My goal is for us to work together on a plan that helps you succeed in your role (We: collaborative approach). Can you share your thoughts on how things have been going?"

This approach allows for a respectful, empathetic conversation focused on a positive outcome for both the employee and the organization. By using the Me-You-We framework, leaders can transform difficult conversations from potential minefields into opportunities for connection and understanding. The approach intends to embody the principles of relatable leadership we've discussed throughout this book—it's respectful, authentic, purpose-driven, and focused on building stronger relationships.

In my consulting practice, I often use role-playing exercises to help leaders practice navigating difficult conversations. Time and again, I've seen how this practical application of the Me-You-We framework can turn potential conflicts into opportunities for growth and understanding.

Addressing Miscommunication and Misunderstandings

Miscommunications and misunderstandings are inevitable in any workplace, but if they are not addressed, they can morph into massive problems. Miscommunications can arise from a variety of sources, including lack of clarity in communication, assumptions, biases, cultural/generational differences, information overload, and differences in communication styles. As a relatable leader, your role is to identify these issues early on and resolve them as efficiently as possible. Here are steps to overcome miscommunication:

Step 1: Identification
Be alert to signs of miscommunication, such as repeated mistakes, frustration among team members, or unexpected conflicts. Remember that these issues may not be immediately obvious.

Step 2: Initiate Dialogue
Take a proactive approach by initiating an open, honest conversation. Start by clarifying the issue without assigning blame. Use phrases like, "I think there might be a misunderstanding about..." rather than "You misunderstood...."

Step 3: Active Listening

Practice active listening, as emphasized in Chapter 5. Give each person involved the opportunity to express their understanding of the situation. Pay attention to words, tone, and body language. Often, miscommunications arise from differences in interpretation rather than the actual words used.

Step 4: Apply the Me-You-We Framework

Me: Acknowledge your own perspective and potential role in the miscommunication.

You: Seek to understand the other person's viewpoint.

We: Work together to clarify the misunderstanding and develop strategies to prevent future occurrences.

Step 5: Forward Planning

Focus on moving forward rather than dwelling on past errors. Collaboratively establish clearer communication protocols or adjust processes to prevent similar issues in the future.

By handling these situations with empathy, clarity, and a solution-focused mindset, you reinforce the principles of relatable leadership and build a more resilient, communicative team.

Adapting Communication Styles to Different Personalities

We have spent a considerable amount of time discussing the differences between generations throughout this book, but we also need to understand how to navigate different personalities. Relatable leaders know that one size does not fit all when it comes to communication. However, this doesn't mean you need to become an expert in every personality type or completely change your communication style for each employee. Instead, the key is developing the skill of "reading the room" and being able to adjust in response to your observations.

Reading the room involves being in tune with the overall energy ("vibe," if you will), engagement levels, and reactions of your audience, whether it's in a one-on-one conversation or a large team meeting. It's about picking up on both verbal and non-verbal cues that indicate how your message is being received and understood. As a keynote speaker, I've learned how important it is to read the room. Every audience is different, but paying attention to subtle cues—like nods of agreement, confused expressions, or the glazed eyes of disengagement—can mean the difference between delivering a message that resonates and falling flat. We can read the same cues one-on-one, and if the other person seems hesitant to speak, you might need to create more space for them to share their thoughts.

This approach allows you to remain authentic while still being flexible and responsive to your team's needs. Remember, the goal is not to become a chameleon but to develop a flexible communication toolkit that allows you to adapt your approach based on the situation and the people involved.

Leaders can maintain the environment of respect and trust they worked so hard to cultivate by being aware of and addressing these common communication pitfalls as they arise.

BREAKING DOWN SILOS

The term "silo" comes from grain silos, designed to separate different types of grain on farms. In organizations, it's used as a metaphor for the separation between different departments or teams.[3] Research has shown that this division has a negative impact on customer outcomes, innovation, efficiency, and overall performance.[4] A survey on collaboration revealed that 83 percent of companies experience silos, and 97 percent of respondents agreed that these silos had an adverse effect on their organizations' success.[5]

Siloed workplaces manifest in various ways. When teams operate in isolation, they create knowledge vacuums. There are missed opportunities to share experience, ideas, and expertise. Teams end up tackling the same challenges, wasting time and resources. Complex problems remain unsolved. Perhaps most harmful, silos breed a culture of division. Teams can become resentful and frustrated, eroding morale. Siloed organizations don't just separate teams—they fracture the organization's potential.

Relatable leaders understand that breaking down silos is necessary to create a truly efficient and productive work environment. We can overcome a divided workplace by focusing on four main areas: creating cross-functional collaboration, aligning goals across departments, developing a culture of knowledge sharing, and implementing effective project management across teams.

Fostering Cross-Functional Collaboration

Cross-functional collaboration is integral to breaking down silos. It involves bringing together individuals from different departments or teams to leverage strengths and work toward common

---

3   The Vocabularist. (2015, June 30). How did "silo" get to mean something else? *BBC News.* https://www.bbc.com/news/blogs-magazine-monitor-33273707

4   De Waal, A., Weaver, M., Day, T., & Van Der Heijden, B. (2019). Silo-busting: Overcoming the greatest threat to organizational performance. *Sustainability, 11*(23), 6860. https://doi.org/10.3390/su11236860

5   Ibid.

goals. Organizations improve problem-solving, decision-making, and innovation by encouraging collaboration across departments. Additionally, cross-functional collaboration can increase engagement and a sense of solidarity within an organization.

Here are some strategies that help to foster cross-functional collaboration:

1. Create a dream team. Determine what projects or undertakings can benefit from cross-functional brain power and create a specific team for the project.

2. Hold regular team-building activities. Organize events that bring together employees from different teams. Ensure they are connecting with those outside of their immediate department.

3. Implement job shadowing. Encourage employees to spend time observing and learning from colleagues in different departments to create understanding.

4. Establish a mentorship marketplace. Create a platform where employees can offer or seek mentorship across departmental lines, creating a transfer of knowledge.

5. Design collaborative workspaces. For in-office organizations, reconfigure office layouts to integrate multiple departments. Sharing common space can lead to spontaneous interactions and relationship building.

6. Rotate meeting leadership. Have different departments take turns leading company-wide meetings. This gives each team a chance to showcase their work and become more familiar with the entirety of the organization.

7. Implement a "No Silo" policy. Explicitly discourage siloed thinking and behavior, making cross-departmental collaboration a KPI for all employees.

Here's an example of a cross-functional success story: Procter & Gamble has utilized cross-functional teams to drive innovation for decades. When developing a new product, P&G brings together teams from research and development, marketing, manufacturing, and supply chain management.[6] They also maintain a program—Connect + Develop—that collaborates outside of their walls as well. Integrating supplies, academia, and entrepreneurs to drive innovation led to the development of products like the Swiffer and Febreze.

Aligning Goals Across Departments

In previous chapters, we've explored the importance of a shared organizational purpose and how important it is to clearly communicate goals; however, in relation to breaking down silos, aligning goals across departments requires a bit more. It's not just about having a common overall mission but also about making sure that the specific goals of each department complement and support *one another* as well as the company.

One infamous example of what happens when goals are misaligned across departments is the American retailer Sears. In 2008, Sears executives revealed a plan that would pit managers and divisions against one another. Each department—such as appliances, clothing, and automotive—would be run and treated as a separate business unit with its own profit and loss statements.

6   Viindoo. (2023, November 18). Cross functional collaboration: Best practices & Examples. *Viindoo*. https://viindoo.com/blog/business-management-3/cross-functional-collaboration-2027

They believed they would find efficiency and success through competition versus collaboration. "The bloodiest battles took place in the marketing meetings, where different units sent their CMOs to fight for space in the weekly circular. These sessions would often degenerate into screaming matches. Marketing chiefs would argue to the point of exhaustion."[7] Instead of creating a cohesive, customer-focused strategy, it led to a fragmented organization. Pundits believe that Sears' siloed approach contributed to its decline, with the company filing for bankruptcy in 2018.[8]

While Sears serves as a warning, many organizations have implemented strategies that promote cooperation across departments instead of rivalry. The answer lies in leadership encouraging departments to view their goals as interconnected pieces of a larger puzzle rather than isolated objectives. Here are several effective strategies:

1. Create interdependent goals. Develop goals within departments where the objectives require collaboration to achieve. For example, a retail company's goal is to increase traffic and conversions. Both the marketing and sales teams need to work together—marketing needs sales to close deals, and sales relies on marketing to drive qualified leads.

2. Implement a company-wide goal-setting framework. Use systems like OKRs (Objectives and Key Results) to ensure all departmental goals tie back to overall company objectives. For example, a tech company sets a com-

7 Moser, W. (2013, July 19). Sears battles socialism and itself with risky new business model. *Chicago*. https://www.chicagomag.com/city-life/july-2013/sears-battles-socialism-and-itself-with-risky-new-business-model/
8 Ibid.

pany-wide OKR to improve customer satisfaction. The product team's key result is to reduce bug reports by 50 percent, while the customer service team's key result is to decrease response time by 30 percent.

3. Hold regular cross-departmental meetings. Schedule regular meetings where department heads share their goals and progress, allowing others to see how they can support or benefit from each other's work. For example, a manufacturing company holds monthly cross-functional meetings where the production team shares their efficiency improvements, helping the sales team adjust their commitments to customers about delivery times.

4. Reward cross-functional achievements. Design recognition systems that acknowledge and incentivize collaborations amongst departments. For example, a pharmaceutical company offers a significant bonus for successful drug launches, split equally among the research, clinical trials, and marketing teams to encourage collaboration throughout the development process.

By aligning goals and creating a North Star for teams to work toward, organizations can avoid silos and develop teams that are more collaborative, innovative, and effective. This approach nurtures a sense of shared purpose (remember Chapter 7), encourages cross-functional problem-solving, and ultimately leads to better outcomes for the company as a whole. When every department understands how its objectives contribute to the bigger picture, it becomes easier to break down barriers, share resources, and leverage diverse expertise across the organization. Speaking of sharing resources...

Creating a Culture of Knowledge-Sharing

A culture of knowledge-sharing can help break down information silos. When information flows across the organization, it reduces the wasted time and effort of multiple teams working to overcome the same challenge.

Strategies to promote knowledge sharing include the following:

1. Encourage open communication. Once again, open communication has to take centerstage as a core component of a successful organization. As we discussed in Chapter 3, creating an environment where team members feel comfortable sharing their ideas, experiences, and insights will pay off in spades, including through the distribution of knowledge.

2. Implement collaborative tools. There are many internal networks and software programs that work to make information easily accessible to everyone. Tools like Slack, Microsoft Teams, or Confluence can make knowledge-sharing easy and keep teams connected.

3. Create knowledge libraries. Develop a centralized database where vital information, best practices, and lessons learned can be stored.

4. Lead by example. When you model behavior that encourages knowledge-sharing, your teams will follow.

5. Provide training and development. Offer training sessions, workshops, or lunch-and-learns led by employees so that they can share their expertise.

Real-world application: Toyota's Yokoten practice epitomizes knowledge sharing. Yokoten, which roughly translates to "horizontal deployment," is an approach to sharing best practices and information throughout the company. When a problem is solved, or an improvement is made in one area of Toyota, the solution is shared and adapted for use in other areas. The goal is to improve innovation and efficiency throughout the company.

By fostering cross-functional collaboration, aligning goals, and promoting knowledge-sharing, relatable leaders can break down silos and create an organization that is more efficient, integrated, and innovative. These shifts won't only improve business outcomes but also create a better environment for your employees, improving relationships and engagements along the way.

MASTERING REMOTE WORK CHALLENGES

Throughout this book, we've discussed aspects of remote work and how important it is for relatable leaders to adapt to meet the demands of a new workplace paradigm. In Chapter 5, we explored how communication strategies have to evolve in virtual settings. Chapter 3 discussed the importance of trust in hybrid and remote teams. In Chapter 6, we examined how recognition practices can be adapted for remote environments. However, as the workplace continues to evolve, with hybrid and fully remote models continuing to dominate workplace models, we also need to address the unique challenges that remote workplaces can create.

As mentioned previously, 58 percent of teams are working remotely, 55 percent are hybrid, and only 20 percent are entirely in person.[9] This seismic shift post-pandemic has brought with it a new set of hurdles—from maintaining team engagement and leader/employee connection across the distance to ensuring equality regardless of location. The challenges are complicated and complex.

---

9   Hoory, 2023.

In this section, we'll explore the four areas that pose significant challenges in remote work settings: building trust and connection in virtual teams, ensuring equity between remote and in-office workers, combating isolation and burnout, and adapting leadership practices for virtual environments.

Building Trust and Connection

Trust, as we explored extensively in Chapter 3, is the foundation of effective teams. However, cultivating trust in a virtual environment can be difficult. Without face-to-face interactions, those spontaneous break room conversations, and the ability to read body language, creating connections that lead to trust requires extra effort.

In a remote setting, every interaction has to become more intentional. Relatable leaders must double down on transparency and consistent communication, as we discussed in Chapter 5. This goes beyond simply sharing information; it involves creating an environment where team members feel safe to express their thoughts, ideas, and concerns openly, which can be even more challenging to facilitate through screens. Regular check-ins, especially one-on-ones, become even more important. It can be easy to disconnect behind a screen; it's your job to draw them back into the fold.

Virtual team-building activities, while sometimes met with an eye roll, can be helpful in building team cohesion. From virtual coffee chats and online games to remote book clubs, these activities can help bridge the physical distance between team members. Note that these do not always have to be a Zoom call. With Zoom fatigue being a very real condition, other methods for these interactions should be considered. Asynchronous communication tools (gaming apps, Slack, and so on) can be equally helpful in promoting connection without adding to the video call overload.

One of the most important elements of building trust in virtual teams requires a mindset shift in how we measure work and productivity. The emphasis needs to shift to results over visibility. No more "face time" or "butts in seats"—it's about trusting your team to manage their time and workload. While it can feel foreign, focusing on work product and outcomes builds relationships by providing autonomy and demonstrating trust.

Ensuring Equity

Another challenge specific to hybrid and remote teams is creating a level playing field for all employees. Consideration of equity is essential to maintain team cohesion and prevent the creation of the silos we so diligently worked to avoid. The hybrid work model can unintentionally lead to a "two-tier" workforce, where remote workers may feel less valued than those in the office.

The solution to addressing this challenge lies in adopting a "remote-first" mindset, even if your organization isn't fully remote. This means designing processes, meetings, and social interactions with remote workers in mind. A few ideas:

1. For video meetings with both remote and in-person participants, consider having everyone join individually.

2. When brainstorming or collaborating, use digital tools that allow for real-time input from all team members.

3. Create a "virtual water cooler" or a chat channel where team members can have more casual conversations.

4. Rotate meeting times to accommodate different time zones if team members are located across the country/world.

Equity also extends to creating equal access to opportunities, particularly in career advancement. Research shows that fully remote workers tend to get promoted less often than their in-office counterparts—a survey found 42 percent of remote workers got a promotion in 2023, compared to 55 percent of fully in-office workers.[10] This contrast highlights the need for leaders to take a look at their promotion practices and ask themselves: Are there team members being overlooked because of their lack of physical proximity? To address this, relatable leaders should be aware during performance evaluations that some criteria may favor in-office presence. By becoming mindful of potential biases, leaders can ensure all team members have an equal chance of promotion based on merit and not location.

Combating Burnout and Isolation

The potential for increased isolation and burnout is another significant challenge of remote work. Remote workers are twice as likely to feel lonely at work than their office-bound counterparts, with 53 percent of those working virtually saying they feel less connected to colleagues.[11,12] In relation to burnout, a condition explored in Chapter 8, a staggering 67 percent of those who work from home reportedly suffer.[13]

---

10 Tan, H. (2023, December 26). Remote workers are less likely to get promotions and raises, but are happier: Survey. *Business Insider.* https://www.businessinsider.com/remote-workers-less-likely-promotions-raises-happier-wfh-rto-survey-2023-12

11 Callahan, C. (2024, June 26). The loneliness epidemic is undying among remote workers. *WorkLife.* https://www.worklife.news/talent/loneliness-remote-workers/

12 HRO Today. (2024, July 10). Gen Z and remote employees are the loneliest at work. *HRO Today.* https://www.hrotoday.com/news/ticker/gen-z-and-remote-employees-are-the-loneliest-at-work/

13 Tsipursky, G. (2022, October 10). Remote work isn't hurting our mental well-being. The lack of work-life boundaries is. *Fortune.* https://fortune.com/2022/10/10/remote-work-hurting-mental-well-being-work-life-boundaries-careers-bosses-gleb-tsipursky/

To combat these issues, organizations need to take a proactive approach. To prevent isolation, have regular check-ins with remote teams, not just for updates on work but to gauge team members' well-being. Allow the conversations to hold space for discussing challenges, stress levels, and any support needed. Create team-building activities both virtually and periodically in person.

Burnout prevention requires a culture that values work–life balance. This starts at the top—with you as the leader modeling healthy behaviors—respecting off-hours, taking regular breaks, and using vacation time. As we discussed in Chapter 4 on authenticity, leaders who demonstrate vulnerability and share how they handle their own work–life balance can create a more open and supportive environment.

Additionally, providing access to mental health resources can pay dividends. This might involve offering counseling services, subscriptions to wellness apps, or organizing virtual wellness activities like group meditation or yoga sessions. Encourage the use of these resources by normalizing conversations about mental health and well-being within your team.

Remember that combating isolation and burnout in remote settings is an ongoing process. Regularly seek feedback from your team about what's working and what isn't. Be prepared to adjust your strategies as needed. The goal is to create a remote work environment that not only maintains productivity but also supports the overall well-being and job satisfaction of your team members. By prioritizing connection, work–life balance, and mental health, you can help your remote team thrive, even in the face of these challenges.

Overcoming Communication Barriers

While we've explored communication challenges earlier in this chapter, relatable leaders must also recognize the need to adapt their communications for virtual teams. Remote and hybrid work can lead to communication breakdowns due to a lack of face-to-face interaction. In a physical office, leaders can often sense the mood of their team and pick up on non-verbal cues. This empathetic and intuitive approach becomes far more difficult in a virtual environment, where interactions are often limited to black-and-white messages and calls with or without video. As we discussed in Chapter 5, effective communication is crucial for relatable leadership, and potential problems are amplified in virtual settings.

Here are some tips for optimizing communication for virtual teams:

1. Utilize multiple communication channels. As discussed in Chapter 5, adapting your communication style to different mediums is essential. Leverage a mix of video conferencing, chat platforms, and email to cater to various communication needs and preferences.

2. Be mindful of tone. Written communication can sometimes come across as impersonal or be easily misinterpreted. Aim for clarity and warmth in messages, and when in doubt or discussing a stressful topic, opt for a video call.

3. Use visual aids. In virtual environments, visual tools such as presentations, diagrams, and screen-sharing can help when discussing complicated ideas and projects and make sure everyone is on the same page.

4. Establish clear communication norms and expectations. Set guidelines for response times, etiquette during meetings, and how communication channels should be utilized.

5. Encourage open and transparent communication. Create an environment where team members feel safe to ask questions, express thoughts, and share concerns. A psychologically safe environment (as discussed in Chapter 4) is imperative when leading a remote team.

With these strategies, relatable leaders can overcome communication barriers in remote and hybrid work environments and create a cohesive unit from afar.

RE-ENGAGING DISENGAGED EMPLOYEES

The challenge of disengaged employees is one that relatable leaders cannot afford to overlook. We have spent a good percentage of this book covering elements of leadership that will intentionally lead to an engaged team, for good reason. According to Gallup, disengaged employees cost the world $8.8 trillion in lost productivity.[14] Employee engagement had actually been on the rise for the past decade, but the pandemic caused a stall in that trend, with currently 32 percent of employees being fully engaged at work.[15] Unengaged teams lead to reduced productivity, innovation, and overall morale. Yet, with the right approach, re-engaging disconnected team members is possible and can revive a struggling organization.

The first step is awareness. Maybe it's a team member who used to be enthusiastic and invested but is now barely participating in meetings. Maybe it's a top performer who is now hovering around average. It could be the team member who has become

14 Pendell, R. (2023, September 11). Employee engagement strategies: Fixing the world's $8.8 trillion problem. *Gallup.* https://www.gallup.com/workplace/393497/world-trillion-workplace-problem.aspx

15 Harter, J. (2024, July 26). US employee engagement inches up slightly after 11-Year low. *Gallup.* https://www.gallup.com/workplace/647564/employee-engagement-inches-slightly-year-low.aspx

increasingly negative and finds fault with everything. In my experience, a single incident isn't cause for alarm, but when there becomes a collection of red flags, the answer is evident—your team is disengaged.

Xavier, a sales director, approached me after a keynote on team building. His face relayed his concern and stress before his words could. "I would love your advice on my team," he began. "They used to be great. High performing, worked together well, I really feel like everyone was sailing in the same direction," Xavier shared. "What's happening now?" I asked.

Xavier sighed heavily, his eyes scanning the floor. "They just seem…off. Less motivated, less engaged. Some days, it feels like I'm pulling teeth just to get them to respond to emails."

I nodded, understanding his frustration. "Have you considered what might be causing this shift?" I asked. Xavier paused for a moment, his brow furrowed. "I've thought about it," he replied. "Maybe it's the new project. It's been a lot of work, and they're all feeling stretched thin."

Xavier went on to explain, "We've been working on this major new client project for the past few months. It's a lot. At first, everyone was excited—it was a challenge. Lately, though, I've noticed a change. Deadlines are being missed, and the quality of work isn't up to our usual standards."

"Have you checked in on them? Asked them what's going on?" I replied.

"Well, no," he admitted. "I've been so focused on meeting the project deadlines. I guess I assumed they'd come to me if there were any problems."

"Understood," I replied. "Let's talk about some strategies to re-engage your team and get to the root of the issue."

We spent the next hour discussing how Xavier could reconnect with his team and reignite their motivation. We covered the importance of individual check-ins, recognizing and celebrating small wins, and realigning the team's day-to-day work with the larger purpose of the project.

A few weeks later, Xavier reached out to let me know the strategies worked. The stress of the project was still there, but the open communication and recognition had completely shifted morale.

Mark's story highlights the importance of staying in tune with your team's engagement levels. It's easier to address waning engagement than reignite a completely disengaged team. To avoid completely disengaged employees, relatable leaders need to be aware of the signs of a disengaged team, which can include:

- Decreased productivity
- Lack of initiative
- Lowered participation
- Increased sick days or late arrivals
- Negative attitude
- Increased conflict

However, recognizing these signs is only the first step. To effectively re-engage employees, relatable leaders must dig deeper to understand the root causes of disengagement so that they can prevent them in the future. Let's explore some of the common reasons why employees become disengaged:

- Lack of clear expectations
- Insufficient feedback
- Lack of recognition
- Poor work–life balance

- Inadequate support/resources/leadership
- Interpersonal conflict
- Feeling undervalued or unheard
- Misalignment with company values

Identifying the root cause is the first step, but the next challenge lies in addressing them effectively. With the signs and causes of disengagement now clear, let's delve into practical strategies that relatable leaders can use to re-engage their teams.

1. Conduct one-on-one check-ins. Have open, honest conversations with disengaged employees to understand their specific concerns and challenges.

2. Provide meaningful feedback. Offer constructive feedback and recognition regularly, not just during annual reviews.

3. Offer growth opportunities. Work with employees to create personalized development plans that align with their career aspirations and company needs.

4. Empower through autonomy. Give employees more control over their work, allowing them to make decisions and take ownership of projects.

5. Reconnect to purpose. Help employees see how their work contributes to the larger organizational mission and impacts others.

6. Address work–life balance. Be flexible with scheduling where possible and encourage healthy boundaries between work and personal life.

7. Improve communication. Ensure transparent, consistent communication about company goals, changes, and expectations.

8. Foster a positive work environment. Promote team-building activities and create opportunities for social connections among colleagues.

By implementing these strategies, relatable leaders can not only re-engage employees but also create a work environment that naturally prevents disengagement. A fully engaged workforce isn't just more productive; it's more innovative, resilient, and, ultimately, more fulfilled. As relatable leaders, there are few things more rewarding than seeing our team members rediscover their passion and purpose, knowing we played a part in rekindling that spark.

Note to readers: To help you assess engagement levels and identify areas for improvement in your organization, refer to the Engagement Survey provided in the Resources section at the end of this book. This survey covers all key aspects of relatable leadership discussed throughout these chapters and can be a valuable tool in your leadership journey.

FINAL THOUGHTS

Throughout this chapter, we've explored various challenges that leaders face—from communication pitfalls and organizational silos, to the complexities of remote work and the struggle of re-engaging disengaged employees.

The key takeaway is that these hurdles, while stressful, are also opportunities for growth and improvement. By addressing communication issues head-on, we strengthen the connections within our teams. In breaking down silos, we create the opportunity to accelerate innovation and improve collaboration. As we adapt to remote work environments, we learn new ways to engage. And in re-energizing disengaged employees, we are able to preserve the teams we worked so hard to build.

Leadership is not about having all the answers, and it's certainly not about perfection. The path forward may not always be smooth, but with a relatable leader at the helm, teams can navigate any waters.

CONNECTION CATALYSTS

Reflect on a recent obstacle your team faced. How did you approach it? What would you do differently using the principles of relatable leadership?

_____

_____

_____

_____

Identify a silo in your organization. Create a cross-functional task force to tackle a shared challenge, bringing together members from different departments.

_____

_____

_____

_____

Conduct an anonymous survey asking team members to identify the most significant obstacles they face in their daily work. Use the results to prioritize which hurdles to address first.

_____

_____

_____

_____

CHAPTER 11

Future of Leadership

"The only thing that is constant is change." —Heraclitus

Throughout the course of this book, my hope is that it's become clear that relatable leadership, at its core, is about creating a culture of connection. An environment where...

- Every team member feels seen, heard, and valued.
- Respect forms the foundation of all meaningful workplace interactions
- Trust builds the bridges that allow ideas and innovation to flow.
- Clear communication opens the doors to higher levels of understanding.
- Recognition motivates and engages employees across generations.
- Individual purpose aligned with organizational goals can unlock unprecedented levels of commitment and creativity.

Relatable leadership is about tapping into our shared humanity, recognizing that behind every job title is a human being with unique experiences, aspirations, and potential. And when we are able to unite those individuals by meeting their needs and showing up as the leader they are looking for and deserve, magic happens.

As we look forward to the future of work, it's clear that human connection remains the priority. While technology will continue to advance rapidly, with today's artificial intelligence likely unrecognizable tomorrow, the human element driving organizational success remains constant. Human connection, communication, and purpose will become more important than ever. In this final chapter, we'll explore how the foundations of relatable leadership we've built together can be utilized to navigate the exciting (but often uncertain) waters that lie ahead.

CHANGING NATURE OF WORK

As we look to the future of leadership, it's clear that work itself is undergoing a major transformation. The Monday to Friday, nine to five model is becoming obsolete. Flexible and creative ways of working have taken its place, and the format continues to evolve. From global pandemics forcing organizations to recognize the potential within remote work to the innovations of technology, where we work is changing just as much as *how* we work. Relatable leaders need to understand and adapt to continue to drive engagement and achieve their goals.

Balancing Act: Fostering Flexibility While Maintaining Productivity and Culture

As organizations grapple with these changes, a challenge emerges: how to balance the desire for flexibility with the need for productivity and a strong company culture. Flexibility is king, with 67 percent of remote, 68 percent of hybrid, and 49 percent of in-person workers prioritizing adaptable work arrangements.[1] Workplace flexibility was ranked as the highest non-salary compensation element.[2] The COVID-19 pandemic served as a catalyst for flexible work, but what began as an emergency response to an unprecedented situation has become a permanent shift. Work is now something we do—not somewhere we go.

Flexible work has many benefits—improved work-life balance, reduced commutes, and broader talent pools, to name a few. However, as we've explored previously, a geographically diverse team can lead to challenges in communication, collaboration, and culture. Leaders need to work to find a balance between offering employees the flexibility they so clearly desire and making sure productivity and cohesion do not suffer.

In some cases, organizations require a return to the office. Others are embracing fully remote models. Many are adopting hybrid approaches, where employees are in the office two to three days per week and working from home. However, it's important to recognize that the flexibility employees are seeking isn't always only about location. There are ways to give all employees more flexibility at work, including:

- Flexible hours: Allow employees to adjust their start and end times to better fit their schedules and work during their peak productivity hours.
- Condensed workweeks: Offer the option to work longer days in exchange for a shorter workweek, for example, four ten-hour days instead of five eight-hour days.

1   The Conference Board. (n.d.). Survey: US employees prioritize workplace flexibility as a key component of compensation. *The Conference Board.* https://www.conference-board.org/press/workplace-flexibility

2   Ibid.

- Job sharing: Split the responsibilities of one full-time position between two part-time employees
- Unlimited PTO with results: Trust employees to manage their own time off as long as their work is completed.

Offering flexible arrangements such as these can provide many benefits to employees associated with remote work while having the best of both worlds with in-office face time. The most successful organizations will likely be those that can strike a balance between structure and flexibility, leveraging the benefits of in-person collaboration while also embracing the advantages of more flexible work arrangements. The key is to approach flexibility with an open mind. What works for one team or company may not work for another. Seek feedback, monitor performance metrics, and be prepared to adjust as needed.

Well-Being at Work

The nature of work has changed and continues to evolve, and so does how employees view work. While employees may have previously been content with a clear separation between work and personal life, today's workforce increasingly seeks integration and balance between the two. Employees want their workplaces to support not just their professional growth but their overall quality of life.

For relatable leaders, this focus on well-being is both a challenge and an opportunity. It requires a more holistic approach to leadership, one that considers the whole person rather than just the employee. Leaders must be attuned to signs of stress or burnout, create psychologically safe environments where employees feel comfortable discussing their well-being, and model healthy behaviors themselves.

Research consistently shows that employees who feel supported in their overall well-being are more engaged, productive, and satisfied at work.[3] As we move forward, the most successful organizations will likely be those that can effectively integrate well-being into their culture, seeing it as a fundamental aspect of how work gets done. Relatable leaders will play an indispensable role in this integration through supporting initiatives and working to create an environment that promotes employees thriving, both personally and professionally.

LEADERSHIP IN A DIGITAL-FIRST WORLD

We are living in a rapidly evolving digital age. New technologies are reshaping our work, our homes, and our relationships. Both businesses and individuals are becoming more and more reliant on technology; as a result, leadership needs to transform as well. Relatable leaders need to be able to balance between embracing new technologies and maintaining the human touch, which is essential to being an effective leader.

Between the time this book was written and published, AI will have already evolved significantly, with new capabilities rolling out at a staggering pace. This rapid advancement has and will continue to reshape businesses worldwide. AI has and will continue to provide both opportunities and challenges for leaders. Relatable leaders need to learn how to adapt to the changes and develop a strategy to integrate AI into their organizations in a way that helps increase productivity.

---

3   Davenport, L. J., Allisey, A. F., Page, K. M., LaMontagne, A. D., & Reavley, N. J. (2016). How can organizations help employees thrive? The development of guidelines for promoting positive mental health at work. *International Journal of Workplace Health Management, 9*(4), 411–427. https://doi.org/10.1108/ijwhm-01-2016-0001

One of the aspects of integrating AI is learning how it can support rather than replace human capabilities. I have heard many iterations of the idea that AI will not replace your job, but someone who uses AI will. There are many areas where leaders can encourage the use of AI to improve efficiency and productivity, from data analysis and pattern recognition to ideation and content creation. By showing teams that AI is a tool that can empower employees rather than a threat to their jobs, leaders can help alleviate fears and resistance.

It should be noted that the ethical implications of AI cannot be overlooked. This includes potential biases in AI algorithms, issues with data privacy that continue to evolve, and potential impact on workforce dynamics. Awareness of these issues and continuing to stay on top of changes is required.

Leaders also need to understand the disruption AI can bring to existing workflows and processes. Change can be challenging to some teams, and it is important to not only understand potential frustrations but to clearly communicate why the changes are being made. This includes training around best practices and ensuring that employees have the resources and support they need to adapt to the new tools. By actively involving the team in the transition, addressing concerns, and emphasizing the long-term benefits, leaders can help prevent many of the potential issues that integrating AI can cause.

The most successful leaders will be those who can harness the power of AI while maintaining the human connections and emotional intelligence that are at the heart of relatable leadership. By embracing AI as a tool to enhance rather than replace human capabilities, leaders can drive innovation, improve efficiency, and create more engaging and productive work environments for their teams.

Beyond AI, leaders must also contend with other digital trends that are reshaping the workplace. Virtual and augmented reality technologies are opening new possibilities for remote collaboration and training. Relatable leaders need to stay informed about these developments as well and consider how they can be leveraged to create connections amongst teams and improve performance.

EVOLVING WORKFORCE DEMOGRAPHICS

As we've discussed throughout this book, leadership is continuously evolving, and so are our teams. The generational landscape is changing and will continue to rapidly shift, with Gen Z and millennials soon becoming the predominant workforce. As shared previously, by 2030, these two younger generations are projected to make up 64 percent of the workforce, with millennials alone accounting for 41 percent. This demographic shift will significantly influence workplace dynamics, leadership expectations, and organizational cultures. This evolving workforce brings new challenges and opportunities, for example:

Gen Z and the digital revolution: Leadership will likely continue to become more tech-savvy to meet Gen Z at work. We may see the rise of leadership strategies that prioritize virtual collaboration and provide real-time feedback. Communication will likely shift toward more frequent, informal, and online modes. The emphasis will continue to increase toward purpose-driven work and leadership with missions at the front and center.

Millennials moving into leadership roles: Millennials, now in their late twenties to early forties, are stepping into leadership positions in record numbers. They are shifting management styles and organizational priorities. Work–life balance will likely become a core leadership principle, with flexible work arrangements becoming the norm rather than the exception. Purpose and impact will be at the forefront of leadership strategies, with increased focus on sustainability, social responsibility, and ethical business practices similar to the desires of their younger counterparts.

Gen X bridging traditional and new leadership approaches: Gen X, often overlooked in generational discussions, plays an important role in bridging traditional leadership styles with newer, more flexible approaches. Cross-generational mentoring programs could become a key leadership tool, facilitating knowledge exchange and fostering innovation through diverse perspectives.

Baby boomers' continued influence and expertise: Despite the influx of younger generations, boomers continue to play a significant role in the workforce. Leadership strategies will need to adapt to leverage the expertise of baby boomers in new ways. We might see the creation of roles that focus on strategic guidance and mentorship rather than day-to-day management. Leadership development programs may expand to include "legacy planning," helping experienced leaders effectively transfer knowledge and prepare for evolving career paths.

As we've discussed throughout this book, each generation has its own set of values, work styles, and expectations. Leaders must do their best to nurture understanding and respect among team members of different generations. By embracing the strengths of each generation and adapting to evolving generational mixes, leaders can create dynamic, inclusive workplaces that leverage the full potential of their teams.

DEIB: THE FOUNDATION OF FUTURE-READY LEADERSHIP

We cannot discuss the future of leadership without the importance of diversity, equity, inclusion, and belonging (DEIB). Diversity at work refers to differences between coworkers based on characteristics including, but not limited to, age, race, gender, and background.[4] As we have covered, our workforce is highly diverse generationally and is becoming more diverse racially and among genders.[5]

It's critical to note that DEIB is a complex, nuanced, and constantly evolving field. While this section aims to highlight its importance in future leadership, it's crucial to recognize that true expertise in this area comes from dedicated DEIB professionals, researchers, and those with lived experiences. As such, the insights shared here should be viewed as a starting point for further exploration and learning rather than definitive guidance.

---

4   Guillaume, Y. R., Dawson, J. F., Otaye-Ebede, L., Woods, S. A., & West, M. A. (2015). Harnessing demographic differences in organizations: What moderates the effects of workplace diversity? *Journal of Organizational Behavior, 38*(2), 276–303. https://doi.org/10.1002/job.2040
5   Minkin, R. (2023, May 17). Diversity, equity and inclusion in the workplace. *Pew Research Center.* https://www.pewresearch.org/social-trends/2023/05/17/diversity-equity-and-inclusion-in-the-workplace/

Future leaders must champion diversity, inclusion, and belonging

America is becoming a minority-majority, with groups formerly seen as "minorities" to reach majority status by 2045.[6] Being a champion of DEIB goes beyond simply hiring a diverse workforce. It requires creating an environment where all employees feel valued, respected, and empowered to contribute their unique perspectives and experience a true sense of belonging. While the specific strategies to achieve this will continue to evolve, some approaches include:

1. Actively seeking out and listening to diverse voices in decision-making processes

2. Challenging unconscious biases in hiring, promotion, and day-to-day interactions

3. Nurturing psychological safety where employees feel comfortable expressing their authentic selves

4. Implementing policies and practices that support equity, inclusion, and belonging across all levels of the organization

5. Creating opportunities for connection and community-building among employees.

Leaders who successfully champion DEIB will not only create more engaged and productive teams but will also be better positioned to attract and retain top talent in an increasingly competitive job market.

---

6   Vespa, J., Medina, L., & Armstrong, D. M. (2020). Demographic turning points for the United States: Population projections for 2020 to 2060. *United States Census Bureau*. https://www.census.gov/library/publications/2020/demo/p25-1144.html

How inclusive leadership and belonging drive innovation

Inclusive leadership isn't just the right thing to do—it's a driver of innovation and performance. Research shows that inclusive leadership promotes psychological safety at both individual and team levels, which in turn boosts innovation throughout the organization.[7] A study by Boston Consulting Group found that companies with above-average diversity within their leadership reported innovation revenue nineteen percentage points higher than companies with below-average leadership diversity.[8] This boost in innovation is often attributed to:

- Diverse perspectives: Teams with varied backgrounds and experiences bring a wider range of ideas to the table.
- Cognitive diversity: Different thinking styles and problem-solving approaches lead to more robust solutions.
- Challenge to groupthink: Diverse teams where members feel they belong are more likely to voice dissenting opinions, leading to better decision-making.

To harness these benefits, leaders must go beyond surface-level diversity to create an environment where all team members feel empowered to contribute their unique insights and experience a genuine sense of belonging. This requires ongoing learning and adaptation of inclusive leadership behaviors.

---

7   Li, T., & Tang, N. (2022). Inclusive leadership and innovative performance: A multi-level mediation model of psychological safety. *Frontiers in Psychology*, 13. https://doi.org/10.3389/fpsyg.2022.934831

8   Lorenzo, R., Voigt, N., Tsusaka, M., Krentz, M., & Abouzahr, K. (2018). *How Diverse Leadership Teams Boost Innovation*. Boston, MA: The Boston Consulting Group.

Practical considerations for creating a more equitable workplace

Equity goes beyond equal opportunity—it's about ensuring fair access, treatment, and advancement for all employees, recognizing that different groups may need different types of support to achieve equal outcomes. Belonging takes this a step further, ensuring that all employees feel they can be their authentic selves at work and are valued for their contributions.

As leadership practices in this area continue to evolve, future leaders should consider the following approaches while always seeking guidance from DEIB experts and staying attuned to the specific needs of their organization:

1. Data-driven approach: Regularly collect and analyze data on hiring, promotions, compensation, employee satisfaction, and sense of belonging across different demographic groups.

2. Transparent pay practices: Implement clear, objective criteria for determining compensation and regularly audit for pay equity across gender, race, and other demographic lines.

3. Inclusive mentorship and sponsorship programs: Ensure that underrepresented groups have access to mentors and sponsors who can advocate for their career advancement.

4. Equitable access to opportunities: Create systems to ensure that high-visibility projects and growth opportunities are distributed fairly rather than defaulting to insider networks.

5. Accommodations and flexibility: Recognize that employees have different needs and life circumstances. Implement

flexible work arrangements and accommodations that allow all employees to perform at their best and feel supported.

6. Ongoing education: Provide regular training on unconscious bias, inclusive behaviors, and cultivating belonging for all employees.

7. Employee resource groups: Support and empower employee-led groups that can provide community, advocacy, and insights to leadership.

The field of DEIB is vast and constantly evolving. There are many resources available online that allow leaders to seek out perspectives from DEIB professionals to gain a better understanding of DEIB challenges and opportunities.

FINAL (FINAL) THOUGHTS

As we wrap up our discussion of the future of leadership, a few things are abundantly clear—work is rapidly evolving, and the fundamental need for human connection remains unchanged. Throughout this book, we've worked through the essential elements that make a leader genuinely relatable—from building respect and trust to communicating effectively, recognizing achievements, aligning purpose, and motivating teams. We've explored how these principles apply across generations and in various work settings, including the challenges of remote and hybrid environments.

As we've seen in this final chapter, the future of leadership will require an even greater emphasis on adaptability, awareness, and technological savvy. The relatable leader of tomorrow will need to navigate the complexities of AI integration, foster inclusivity in increasingly diverse workplaces, and prioritize employee well-being in new and innovative ways. They will need to balance the efficiencies offered by technology with the irreplaceable value of human interaction and emotional intelligence.

Yet, at its core, relatable leadership will always be about connecting, communicating, and inspiring people. The principles we've explored throughout this book—respect, trust, clear communication, recognition, purpose, and motivation—will remain the bedrock of effective leadership, even as everything around us continues to change.

As you move forward in your leadership journey, remember that being a relatable leader is not about perfection but about continuing to work, grow, and try—your effort counts. It's about creating an environment where every team member feels valued, heard, and empowered to reach their full potential. It's about adapting to new challenges while staying true to the fundamental human needs that drive engagement and success.

The journey to becoming a relatable leader is ongoing. It requires constant reflection, learning, and growth. As you face the challenges and opportunities of the future, I encourage you to return to the principles and strategies we've explored in this book. Remain curious, open-minded, and committed to evolving alongside the changing world of work. By doing so, you'll be well-positioned to lead with empathy, authenticity, and effectiveness in the years to come.

Remember, the future belongs to leaders who can connect, communicate, and inspire across all generations and in all work environments. By embracing the principles of relatable leadership, you're not just preparing for the future—you're helping shape it. As I continue to speak and consult with organizations worldwide, I'm constantly inspired by leaders who embrace these principles of relatable leadership. Their success stories fuel my passion for this work and reinforce the universal applicability of the strategies explored in this book. Here's to your journey as a relatable leader and to the positive impact you'll make on your teams, your organizations, and the world of work as a whole. I believe in you.

CONNECTION CATALYSTS

Consider the diverse demographics of your team. Identify one area where you could improve inclusivity or equity. What specific action can you take this week to make progress?

_____

_____

_____

_____

Reflect on your team's current use of AI tools. How could you better integrate AI to enhance productivity while still maintaining the human touch in your leadership?

_____

_____

_____

_____

Looking ahead to the future of work, what's one potential challenge you foresee for your organization? Outline a preliminary strategy for how you would address this challenge using the principles of relatable leadership.

_____

_____

_____

_____

Reflecting on your leadership journey throughout this book, what has been your most significant insight or area of growth? How do you plan to incorporate this into your leadership practice going forward?

_____

_____

_____

_____

Engagement Survey

As I came to the end of writing *The Relatable Leader*, I realized how many times I recommended surveying your team for feedback and data. It became very clear that it would be valuable to share a survey similar to those we deploy through my consulting firm, The Magnet Method. This resource allows leaders to take a temperature check at the outset and identify areas for improvement. This survey covers all the key aspects of relatable leadership; I encourage you to adapt this survey as needed to fit your organization's specific needs. There are forty-four questions (a homage to my Syracuse University roots or a natural end to the questions? One will never know), and while using it in its entirety could paint a comprehensive picture, you may want to pick and choose those that are most needed to achieve your organization's current goals.

Remember, the true value of this survey lies not just in conducting it, but in how you use the results. Be prepared to act on the feedback you receive, share aggregated results with your team, and develop action plans based on what you learn. This process of seeking feedback, reflecting, and taking action is at the heart of relatable leadership.

Let's dive into the survey questions.

PLEASE RATE EACH STATEMENT ON A SCALE OF 1 TO 5, WHERE:

1 = Strongly Disagree

2 = Disagree

3 = Neutral

4 = Agree

5 = Strongly Agree

Respect and Trust

1. I feel respected by my immediate supervisor.

2. My opinions and ideas are valued by leadership.

3. I trust the leadership of this organization.

4. There is a culture of mutual respect among team members.

5. I feel psychologically safe to express my thoughts and concerns.

Communication

1. My supervisor communicates clearly and effectively.

2. I receive regular and constructive feedback on my performance.

3. Leadership is transparent about important decisions affecting the organization.

4. I feel comfortable approaching my supervisor with questions or concerns.

5. Communication channels in our organization are effective.

Authenticity and Vulnerability

1. My supervisor demonstrates authenticity in their interactions.

2. Leadership is willing to admit mistakes and learn from them.

3. I feel comfortable being my authentic self at work.

4. Our organization values diverse perspectives and experiences.

5. Leaders in our organization show vulnerability when appropriate.

Recognition and Appreciation

1. I receive meaningful recognition for my contributions.

2. Our organization has effective systems for acknowledging employee achievements.

3. My supervisor regularly expresses appreciation for my work.

4. Recognition in our organization feels sincere and personalized.

5. There are opportunities for peer-to-peer recognition.

Purpose and Motivation

1. I understand how my work contributes to the organization's mission.

2. My work feels meaningful and purposeful.

3. Our organization's mission and values align with my personal values.

4. I feel motivated to go above and beyond in my role.

5. Leadership effectively communicates our organization's purpose and goals.

Growth and Development

1. There are clear opportunities for professional growth within the organization.

2. My supervisor supports my professional development.

3. I have access to the resources and training I need to improve my skills.

4. Leadership encourages innovation and new ideas.

5. I feel challenged and stretched in my current role.

Work Environment and Well-being

1. Our organization promotes a healthy work-life balance.

2. I feel supported in managing my workload effectively.

3. The physical or virtual work environment supports my productivity.

4. Our organization takes steps to prevent burnout.

5. I feel that my overall well-being is valued by the organization.

Diversity, Equity, and Inclusion

1. Our organization values diversity in all its forms.

2. I feel that all employees have equal opportunities for advancement.

3. Leadership actively promotes an inclusive work environment.

4. I've never experienced or witnessed discrimination in our workplace.

5. Our organization takes concrete actions to address bias and promote equity.

Open-Ended Questions

1. What is one thing our leadership does well that you'd like to see continued or expanded?

2. What is one area where you think our leadership could improve?

3. How could our organization better support your professional growth and development?

4. Is there anything else you'd like to share about your experience with leadership in our organization?

About the Author

Rachel DeAlto is a communication and relatability expert, media personality, keynote speaker, emcee, and Match Group's Chief Connection Officer. She is also the co-founder of The MAGNET Method, a consulting firm focused on employee engagement.

Rachel maintains a law degree from Seton Hall School of Law, a Master's in psychology from Arizona State University, and an influential social media presence where she shares psychological research updates and practical takeaways on relationship-building, communication, and leadership.

She has appeared as an expert on Lifetime's Married at First Sight and over two hundred national media outlets. Rachel speaks on the power of connection and leadership. She is also the author of *relatable: How to Connect with Anyone Anywhere (Even if It Scares You)*.

Learn more about Rachel and her refreshing relatability at *racheldealto.com*.